# True Tales
# of the
# Truly Weird

Danielle Egnew

Printed in the United States of America
Copyright © 2012 Danielle Egnew

ISBN: 1478181109
ISBN-13: 978-1478181101

Editor: Kristen Coyner
Cover photo: Savannah Stevenson
Cover design: Danielle Egnew

Published by Create Space with permission from
The Call To Light Press
A division of Ave Vox Entertainment Group
15021 Ventura Blvd Suite 843, Sherman Oaks, CA 91403
contact@avevoxentertainment.com

Danielle Egnew, Los Angeles, CA

To the best of the author's ability, the author has recreated experiences,
people, places, and organizations from the author's memory. In order to
protect the privacy of others, the author has changed the names of actual
participants.

# DEDICATION

I dedicate this book to my family, both biological and by choice. May all the storms within be calmed by the Peace above.

I also dedicate this book to those who struggle with their own Psychic abilities, as well as the many reputable paranormal investigators whose work brings clarity to clients in need.

And to all who read this book -- may the only bump in the night be your shins against the coffee table.

# CONTENTS

# PREFACE

As a Psychic and Medium who works in media, it's very important to me to educate the masses on what's really "out there" (so to speak). I feel the more we know as a species the less we have to fear. Fear is the electric fence of the soul. When we are in fear, we only allow ourselves to peak through the fence at the darkness beyond. We speculate about the content of the darkness and in this speculation create grandiose horrors born from the deepest corners of our imagination. We then label these terrifying projections as reality. Yet what if this fear fence were eradicated? What if we no longer feared, but were fascinated, by all things that went bump in the night? Could we then turn the energy of demonization into that of discovery?

I believe we can.

For the past many years, I have been asked: "When are you going to write a book?" Though I've wanted to write a book, the task always fell behind other projects – music, TV, and films. However, no matter how busy I would become with other endeavors, I've started and stopped writing on many spiritual books. At the time, each book seemed to be the correct message for the moment. There are so many areas within the spiritual landscape which are near and dear to my heart that deciding upon one was difficult. I decided the best way to break the authorship ice was to simply tell the truth. To me, there is power in the truth. And there is power in a story. Combine the two and the educational and entertainment value is unparalleled.

I'm drawn to books about people's lives. I want to study their journey and hear their stories. I want to be entertained as well as and educated. And if it's to do with the paranormal – I want to be scared at times, too. I realized that my life in and of itself fit all the above criteria.

It was in writing this book that I was able to truly reflect on the outrageous amount of paranormal encounters I've experienced throughout my lifetime. To be honest, it was a tad jaw-dropping. Yet in actually trying to decide which stories to include in this book, I realized that there are not enough pages to adequately hold every experience I've had. Instead, I've chosen the most diverse – and the weirdest – tales from a broad array of my most bizarre paranormal encounters. It's my hope that in reading this "sample platter of the paranormal" others will allow themselves to feel less alone in their own experiences.

You'll notice that I've changed the names of the (not so) innocent while recounting these true tales. This is for no other reason than to protect the privacy of those who experience these bizarre situations along with me. Not everyone is up for copping to their paranormal experiences. Many of the people mentioned in this book are now surrounded by more conservative cultures or have religious families. Since this is a book of true tales and Hollywood tell-all, it's my wish to honor people's life choices – not rip anyone from the paranormal closet. Those mentioned in this book – and you know who you are -- feel free to "out" yourselves. I just feel that's your choice, not mine.

They say the devil is in the details. I'd offer that the destination is in the details. If we are to get from point A to point B in the paranormal field, we must consider all things: History, mythology, scientific information, spiritual customs, and of course -- first hand experience. When I directed and starred in my paranormal documentary *Montgomery House: The Perfect Haunting*, it was incredibly important to me to include the history of the location. It was within the history that the terror was anchored. So I've included some of the creepiest history you'll find anywhere, right here in this book. Luckily for me, it all just so happened to correspond with my experiences.

*True Tales of the Truly Weird* is my story, from one really weird encounter to the next. Welcome to my life, from that of a young child on. I hope to allow you to see through my eyes what it's like to navigate every day in my spiritual skin so that you may gain clues in how to better to navigate life within your *own* spiritual skin. We are all "psychic": Spiritual beings living a physical existence. It's in how we each use our gifts that defines our purpose in this lifetime.

Now – go get yourself a bowl of popcorn, light some candles, and curl up with this book full of true paranormal tales. Maybe if you're lucky, the wind will whistle through the hollow tress outside, just for effect.

My life is literally -- in your hands. So here we go.

TRUE TALES OF THE TRULY WEIRD

# 1

## IF YOU SEEK IT, IT WILL FIND YOU
### WHERE: BILLINGS, MONTANA
### LOCATION: MOUNTVIEW CEMETERY

Growing up in Montana, there wasn't a lot to do – unless you created the fun yourself. The whole state of Montana has a population of 900,000, and it's the fourth largest state in the union, behind (in order) Alaska, Texas, and California. Considering that the state of Montana is made up of 147,042 square miles, there is one square mile for every 61 people. Now, considering that there are 27,878,400 square feet in a mile, every person in that square mile gets 457,022 square feet of space. In Houston, TX, that square footage would be worth over $2,943,776 with a building value of $21,556,224 for a total property value of $24,500,000.

Too bad it's not in Houston.

Instead, a great deal of Montana is covered in areas that are so inhospitable to live that nothing outside of rattle snakes or grizzly bears attempt to do so. The rest of us were congregated into towns and cities where other humans could be found, and usually, those humans wouldn't try to gnaw off your leg to get through the winter. Well, unless you went east of Miles City, but that's your own problem if you're out knocking around out in Eastern Montana before springtime.

I'm extremely lucky to have grown up where I did. I look around at kids who were raised in larger cities, where there are literally hundreds of things to go do at any given time, from museums to different shopping areas to glorious traveling Broadway shows. And, though I'm sure there is enormous merit in being able to grow up in that environment, I've found that some of my best pals who were reared with "things to do" don't often know what to do unless, well… there are "things" to do.

In Montana, "doing things" took on a whole new creative meaning. Sure, if you were outdoorsy, you could hunt or fish. I wasn't a hunter, but I enjoyed fishing. Yet that activity was only available during three months out of the summer, unless one endeavored into ice fishing, and again – that whole "inhospitable" thing comes to mind. So once the fall rolled in and started blowing that stabbing arctic air straight down from Canada and between the buttons on my jacket – it was time to wrap up one's outdoor adventures.

Consider that living in Montana meant that you had to be at peace with the seasons, as it's a very seasonal place. Like clockwork, we'd have three months of everything: Spring, Summer, Fall, and Winter. Summertime was easy to fill with activities – lots of camping, fishing, hiking, and outdoor music events that rolled well into the evening, where 10:30 pm still held a light twilight blue in the far northern sky long after the sun set. Wintertime was also defined very clearly, either by how much money you had, or how many in-home projects you had to work on. I say that because the folks who had money went skiing, with all the lift and equipment prices, and those of us who didn't would hibernate into the warmth of the house while 3:00 pm brought on the darkness of night in the deep northern winter. As snow piled up outside, I'd write music, or make jewelry, or paint. I'd go wild in the outback known as my own mind. (The weather was much more temperate in there.) If cabin fever set in to the point of not being able to stand the site of our own living room any further, Grandma and Grandpa would toss some sleds or inner tubes in the station wagon and head to the hilly side of the city park, or find some random side of a mountain that was not only void of trees but was far enough away from the road that racing down the hill wouldn't result in being catapulted at the most inopportune time in front of an oncoming semi truck. Sledding was fun until you got too wet, too far from civilization, and then you remembered why snow sports were so much more enjoyable if you had money and could afford the decent snowsuit, warm lodge at the bottom of the mountain, and of course – the toddy to remove the chill.

Springtime was a welcome relief from the three month imprisonment the freezing temperatures would inflict upon every resident of Montana. We'd cut the legs off our jeans at the mere peak of sunshine. Who cares if the icicles were just beginning to drip? As the arctic winds retreated high back into the frozen hell they came from, fifty degrees felt like a nude sprawl on a tropical beach. We'd venture back out to the shopping malls, thrilled to finally snag some fresh produce from the grocery store that didn't taste like the lettuce you'd see on the floor of a prison, or broccoli so brown that you were sure it had some sort of mange that should be reserved for an outdoor cat. Spring meant fishing in the mud and roaring winds that were so ridiculous that the only thing one could do is – literally -- fly a kite. Spring was the ramp-up to Summer, which, for all intents and purposes, was the no-holds-barred time where all Montanans had a free pass to lose their minds in joyful abandon – as long as no one took your land, your cattle, or your gun.

It was Fall that was the holdout.

Fall in Montana is tricky. Of all the seasons, it's the most deceptive. To be honest, it also can be the most depressing, and the most suspenseful. And, it's one of my favorites, in spite of its slightly desperate and convoluted energy. Though I looked forward to the brilliant colors and the crisp smells of fallen leaves, Fall in Montana has the same feeling as riding a roller coaster up to the first drop. With every tick of the chain pulling the cars up to the peak, the rider knows that it is only a matter of time before their gorgeous panoramic view of the illuminated theme park at sunset is mere seconds away from being replaced with a dead plummet that would make any sane person pray for instant death. Just as the impending doom of gravity looms large, the impending doom of deep freeze is right around Fall's corner.

I found Fall in Montana to be much like watching a bomb tick down. Every day – and I mean, every day – signs of the outdoor world shutting down would be made evident. A loss of a degree on the thermometer here and there, more leaves hitting the ground, the sun dipping lower and lower over the horizon, crisp winds beginning to bite; like a rabbit barely left conscious with each squeeze of the python – soon, you were trapped in the dark belly of Winter.

Because one never knew what one was getting with Fall, in a state where every Montanan had 457,022 square feet of space to occupy -- we had to work extra hard to fill our time. So, what better to do than sink into the receding energy of stasis? How better to fill one's time than not to beat 'em, but join 'em, in the celebration of all things dying?

Ergo – Fall in Montana meant ghost hunting.

My childhood buddy "Jake" and I were in our very early twenties and as such, hanging out with a fantastic group of students who attended Rocky Mountain College in Billings, my home town. Though I never was a student there, as college didn't really end up being my thing, this happened to be the same college that both my parents attended. I'd heard countless Rocky Mountain College stories from years gone by and it was a treat to be able to spend time with our friends in the same dorms that I'd heard so much about.

Rocky Mountain College is a prestigious private Christian school and has quite a history, including educating famous students such as 60's folk hero Arlo Guthrie. Established in 1878, it also has the distinct honor of being the oldest college in Montana. As such, its hand-chiseled sandstone block walls hold secrets that have been passed down from one generation to the next -- sordid tales of haunted halls still heavy with the woe of those who had taken their own lives there. Whether these tales were true or not was wildly beside the point. Rocky Mountain College, in the fall, looked creepy, with majestic castle-like facings gripped in the tightening clasp of twisted, dying vines.

If a person wanted to scare themselves, this was the place to do it.

Jake and I had heard tale of one of the campus ghosts, and we decided that we were going to go looking for this creature. The lore went that many moons ago, Mr. Losekamp, a major benefactor to the college, donated money to build Losekamp Hall, the performing arts building, in honor of his wife's love of music and theater. That's the only part of the story that remains consistent. The rest of the story breaks into a trickling vein of reality TV plotlines, but always ends with grief stricken Mr. Losekamp hanging himself in one of the turrets of Losekamp Hall after his wife's untimely death.

Since Jake and I were aware that the college wouldn't leave open the doors to Losekamp Hall after hours -- which of course we were certain was the time when the ghosts would be in residence, don't you know – we made sure to secure a back door so that we could slip in once the sun set. And set it did, to bring in sporadic bursts of raging winds that whipped up the brittle shells of fallen leaves. It was a scene from a John Carpenter movie, the barren trees clacking as the night wind rattled their bony fingers together. We wanted to wait until midnight to start our creepy crusade, but considering the dark of night came on much sooner in the fall, it felt quite late at 10:00 pm. So we went ahead as planned.

We both had a nervous excitement about sneaking into this building after hours that I'm sure eclipsed the thought of actually running into a ghost. Prior to our venture, earlier that day, I made sure to eyeball the building with the intention of scoping out any potential security cameras that may put a damper on our evening's excursion. Thanks to tradition – Rocky Mountain College was void of such tacky wall hangings. In truth, Losekamp Hall could not have had two more respectful snoopers: I was a theater major, and so was Jake, and this was a theater building on the campus. So we had great reverence for the space, even though we snuck in.

Now it's important to note once again that we were ghost hunting in 1991, well before any of the popular paranormal television shows gave demonstration of this pursuit. So in essence, we made it up as we went along, going from room to room with our flashlight, asking the standard questions: Was Mr. Losekamp there? Why did he kill himself? Could he see us? These inane questions are the like that now, I would never ask a spirit (because, hello McFly, of *course* they can see you) -- but hey, I was barely into my twenties, and for all intents and purposes, I really didn't have a grasp of my Psychic abilities yet. So I was pinch-hitting. Luckily, Jake is a Scorpio, and naturally drawn to the mystical, so he was pretty darn effective when it came to spirit communication. To give credit where credit is due, he actually did a better job than I did with his choice of questions for the deceased. So if indeed Mr. Losekamp was hanging around – no pun intended – I'm sure he was happy that Jake was onboard. I say "if" Mr. Losekamp was around because I really couldn't feel anything in Losekamp Hall except for an overwhelming sense of peace.

We wandered around, poking our heads into this hallway and that, only to find a dark, quiet building, except for the startling bursts of fall wind that would roar out of nowhere, rattling the old windows. Finding nothing but peace in the building – and that was no fun -- we both thought it would be a good idea to venture into the theater, as most theaters tend to be haunted. It's common. As theater majors, both Jake and I had encountered different spirits in different theaters across the country – specters of the boards that would move your grease paint make-up from exactly where you put it the night before into a strange stack the next morning, or continually re-hang only one piece of Shakespearean garb in a very odd place, like in the middle of a doorway. There is an enormous amount of energy stored in all live theaters and performance spaces. True performers – actors and singers -- are channels, though many are not aware of this. Theaters then become a hotspot for paranormal activity because one channel after another has let loose all of what they have in the space. Think about it: Actors channel the deepest sorrows and the highest joys of characters, over and over again, day after day, night after night. (No one goes to a play to see a character slog through the emotionally mundane for two hours.) The walls of the theater then store the incredible high resonant vibration of this heated emotion and either create a whirlpool of focused energy -- a vortex – or, the building itself absorbs the performance vibrations and becomes a battery pack from which spirit life may draw energy. Knowing this, Jake and I were sure that if we were to find Mr. Losekamp, he'd be in the theater.

We were on the second floor of the building and as such we stepped onto the theater's balcony, staring at the dark stage below. Rocky Mountain College was initially a Jesuit school that had adopted two other Christian modalities later on, and so Losekamp Hall was adorned with the most gorgeous stained glass windows one could imagine. It was more like standing in a church with a stage up front, rather than an altar. Though I could feel that signature resonant hum that all theaters possess, the only energy that communicated with us – was a quiet peace.

Well…dang.

What was rather remarkable about this peace, however, was that it rendered both Jake and I silent. We both stood in the dark, the wind howling outside and spitting dead leaves at the stained glass windows, captivated by the contrast between the stillness inside and the chaos outside. My memory was instantly drawn to a story told to me by one of my uncles, who had recounted how he had ventured up onto the balcony of Losekamp Hall during his tenure as a student at Rocky Mountain College. While there, he felt an overwhelming sense of peace followed by a Universal Knowingness that he could never quite explain. It was if, for a few precious split seconds, everything in the universe just made sense. There was no fear or worry – only an enlightening awareness of why everything was the way it was, and it all fit perfectly. He went on to explain how this realization was so big, so out of any paradigm that he could explain as a human being who views the world from challenge to challenge, that all he could do was sink into the utter blissful weightlessness of this Awareness, and suspend himself there for a moment. I came to find out later in life that this same experience is often shared by people who are in the presence of angels, or live through a near death experience. It is, in essence, the "feeling" that comes over a person when one is within the presence of God.

I can't say our experience on that theater balcony was as dramatic. But I can say that I understood how my uncle's experience occurred there. It was clear to me that Losekamp Hall was not the place to be if one was seeking creepy crawlies that lurked in the dark.

Jake and I left the building making sure the door locked tightly behind us. We were, after all, adventurers, not pillagers, and we didn't want theft to befall the theater. There was such a stark contrast between the ethers inside and outside, with the stab of Fall winds funneling down our ear canals as Jake leaned against the gusts to ensure the door clicked shut. Once outside, the other-worldly bliss from within blew away in the churning Fall night, and our attention was once more focused on our mission: to find ghosts.

We hopped into my car and drove back to Jake's to reconvene while imbibing on some much needed ghost-hunting fuel: Folgers drip coffee and cinnamon rolls he had made earlier that day. We plotted and strategized our next move. Should we head to Boothill, an historical Montana cemetery within the city limits? Nothing says "bring me a ghost!" like deaths via hanging, snake bite, gunshot or malaria. Named Boothill because a majority of its occupants died with their boots on in either one bizarre Old West way or another, Boothill Cemetery was a field of prickly-pear cactus and weather-worn handmade crosses, now blackened and eroded from the elements. One of its most famous residents was Muggins Taylor, the scout who carried the news of Custer's Last Stand at the Battle of the Little Bighorn to the rest of the world.

The historic cemetery's last burial took place in 1882. Once far away from the town site that provided it's occupants – Coulson, the rough and tumble but ill-fated boomtown across the river -- Boothill was now awkwardly nestled directly below the low flight path of the Billings Logan International Airport, and wedged between an Applebee's and the appropriately-titled "Boothill Inn", a several story Super-8-adjacent motel. (Again, nothing says "Stay here!" like a motel touting the fact that an old rotted graveyard is thirty paces away.)

Even we weren't sure that we wanted to insult Boothill further with a ghost hunt.

In the very least, its occupants – former Coulson residents – really did see themselves as movers and shakers in their time; sure that Coulson would be the largest city in Montana due to its River Boat port. So perhaps being forever interned within the commercial district of what came to be the largest city in Montana – Billings – wasn't so bad for these folks? Personally, it would depress the heck out of me. But Coulson residents weren't the usual lot. **In fact, Coulson's story was a little twisted.**

Founded in 1877, the Sheriff of Coulson was Liver-Eating Johnston. And no, I did not make that up. Feel free to Google this historical wackadoodle. Liver-Eating Johnston was a big guy, six feet tall and over two hundred pounds. He was a Civil War Naval Officer turned Gold Miner turned Mountain Man who took a Native American wife. In 1847, his wife was killed by Crow Indians and Johnston was set ablaze with hatred for the Crow tribe. This hatred fueled a 12 year rampage against the tribe that would involve him cutting out and eating the liver of each man he killed. Not only was the act frighteningly barbaric, but it was a direct insult to the Crow, as by their customs, it reduced them to "prey". The Crow would gut their animal kills in the field and eat the raw livers on the spot because they felt it passed on to them the life force of the beast. So to have one of their own devoured by Liver-Eating Johnston meant to have their life forces trapped within an enemy. It was pretty raw. (Again, no pun intended.)

It's even said that Liver-Eating Johnston was ambushed by a group of Blackfoot warriors who planned to sell him to the Crow, thinking they could get a pretty penny for this desecrater. As was customary by the Blackfoot, they stripped him to the waist and tied him with sinew lashings, posting a young guard outside. Johnston, not one to be turned over to a tribe who he'd been eating, chewed through the straps, knocked his guard flat with a crack to the face, then scalped the guard with his knife. As if that weren't enough, (because apparently Liver-Eating Johnston was very thorough), he quickly sawed off one of his scalped captor's legs. He then made a break for the woods, surviving a two hundred mile journey by eating – wait for it -- the Blackfoot captor's leg, until he reached an outlaying cabin belonging to a trapping buddy.

Yep. This guy was the Sheriff of Coulson, Montana.

The best part of Coulson was the fact that it was the extinct predecessor to Billings. Billings city limits are defined by natural boundaries -- flanked on it's north by a set of sandstone cliffs called The Rimrocks beneath which Boothill cemetery sits, and flanked on the south by the mighty Yellowstone River, the very last – and only -- major water arterial left in the nation that remains undammed. But back in Coulson's day – Billings was nothing but a valley across the river called the Clark's Fork Bottom.

Coulson was a town the things of which classic westerns were made. Breaking in the Montana territory, this raucous settlement sat in the shadow of the 800 foot tall Sacrifice Cliff, where pre-westernized Crow Indian warriors would ride over the edge offering their lives to the Great Spirit in hopeful exchange for a blessing of tribal deliverance from the onslaught of Smallpox brought in on blankets by disingenuous cavalry traders. (Germ warfare started early in this country.) As was the habit of the white man, Coulson was, of course, erected right at the base of this Crow Indian holy site, known as Four Dances, and built on top of who knows how many bones of Brave and Horse with no respect for the Native traditions. The Crow Indians had all since been scooped up onto their reservation 50 miles south, and were considered savages anyway, later being harshly catalogued in the 1912 edition of the Encyclopedia Brittanica as "ugly" and "not" intelligent.

Ah, Caucasian hubris.

Caucasians did love their opinions, and their capitalism. Commercial sponsorship started early in Montana, which made sense since the state was acquired into the union due to the commercial value of its mineral rights, coal, oil, and never-ending sea of bloodied Buffalo pelts. In the spirit of such sponsorship, Coulson was named after the Coulson Packet Company that operated River Boats between St. Louis and ports of call in Montana via both the mighty Yellowstone and Missouri rivers. In my lifetime, I'm waiting for a city in Indonesia to be named Nike. But I digress.

Coulson was a hot and happening place for the day, and it bragged that it was going to be the next big western hub. A lumber mill was erected and a dentist took up residence to deal with gunfights. (You read that correctly.) The dentist was the doctor back in the day. It was the birth of multi-tasking, to be followed shortly thereafter by the Judge-Postmaster-Sheriff. Coulson became a far-west Oasis, doubling as the local stage stop and area post office. It was not only the River Boat port, but once news of the expanding railroad spread, the money-blinded townsfolk were positive they would be bathed in wealth. As reported by the Coulson Herald, the entire population of 50 stripped naked and went skinny dipping in the Yellowstone River to celebrate this anticipated avalanche of cash.

Sidebar: This nasty "swimming in the river" gig is a tip-off for who we are dealing with here. The Yellowstone River is a wide and deep fury of freezing and churning water. Originating at 5,600 feet in Yellowstone Park and flowing north to 1,800 feet, meeting the Missouri River 692 miles later, the river changes personality dramatically. Though not as wide or as long as the Mississippi, the Yellowstone River's dangerous bite comes from the fact that it's an enormous amount of water flowing at a much steeper grade. By the time the Yellowstone has raged through the mountains, ripping over falls like the 105 foot drop at Natural Bridge, the water by Billings – or then, Coulson -- is so muddy that even in three inches, you can't see the bottom. Giant dislodged cottonwood branches fly down the river like invisible missiles, hidden in the murky water to become the treacherous end for many a boat. The Yellowstone is so big and so powerful that there are three different current flows within the river, creating "three rivers" running on top each other, at once. Called a "convection current", the unique flow of the water forms deep holes in the riverbank, earning the waterway a worldwide reputation for stellar trout fishing. However, the Yellowstone River would just as soon use it's convection current to suck you under into the piles of decaying deadfall below as share it's signature 10 pound Cutthroat Trout. So what exactly *is* a deadly convection current, you may ask? Well it goes something like this:

Freezing water flowing from glaciers at 10,000 feet feed the river. The colder the water, the more dense, and it sinks to the bottom of the riverbed, flowing at a faster rate down the steep grade because it's heavier. Downriver, the slightly warmer water trickling in from feeder streams is less dense, so it floats on top of the freezing bottom layer that's racing beneath it. This creates a "second river" that flows at a slower pace. Dangerous invisible whirlpool currents are generated several feet below the surface as the "two rivers" fight against one another. Meanwhile, on the surface, the wide mass of water is warmed by the sun, creating a "third river" which meanders more slowly on top than the "two rivers" rushing below at different speeds. The surface of the Yellowstone River is peppered with tiny swirls created from this complex convection current -- the only indicator that anything below is different that what you see on top. Diving into the Yellowstone River is much like walking into quicksand: The surface of the path looks no different until you step on it, instantly sinking to your knees, realizing that what looked like solid land was pure mush camouflaged by dirt and gravel simply floating on top. I've known people who were swimming in the Yellowstone that have witnessed someone less than three feet from them being sucked under, as if violently snatched below the surface by a great white shark. The unfortunate swimmer happened upon one of these multi-layered currents, and much like a riptide in the ocean, they were instantly vacuumed to the bottom of the deep riverbed by one of the multi-current whirlpools. Now trapped in the fast-moving freezing dominant current below, they become pinned beneath millions of cubic tons of water racing above them, unable to kick off from the bottom to reach the surface, only to end up crushed against deadfall downstream to drown.

As you can see, anyone who swims naked in the Yellowstone River to "celebrate" – has problems.

As history would have it, all of these problems finally came home to roost as Coulson's dreams of wealth through Western Expansion came to a crashing halt. The Northern Pacific Railroad decided to bypass the River Boat port in favor of two odd plots of land across the river that they could actually get their hands on, located in the Clark's Fork

Bottom. These two haphazard plots became Billings, and though Coulson hung in there, even being attached to Billings for a time via trolley – Coulson finally met the fate of countless Old West boom towns, shrinking into humbling obscurity as the wealth and population headed directly across the river. So close, but yet, so far.

Oddly, the City of Billings has never built anything on the old Coulson location, and it remains a city park to this day. Considering the value of land in Billings, this is a statement. I think, in some way, Billings is attempting to show some respect for its mother town site by allowing her to lay in rest, peacefully. Someone had to be allowed to rest peacefully. Lord knows it wasn't going to be the poor saps buried under the neon light of Applebee's, up on Boothill.

Neon or not, as budding paranormal investigators, a cemetery of some sort seemed like our best bet for finding a ghost late in the Fall night. Plus, let's not rule out the pure scary factor. Jake and I felt like we'd been ripped off, having stood in the peace of Losekamp Hall for a few hours, and we sere seeking something truly terrifying. That was the point of ghost hunting, right? (Ah, youth.) So, upon finishing up several delectable homemade cinnamon rolls, because one needs to make sure to load up on the carbs before venturing out into the chilly Montana air, Jake and I bundled up once again and turned our sites on our next most respectful conquest: Mountview Cemetery.

Mountview wasn't very far from Jake's house, and it was a much larger cemetery than the historical yet decrepit Boothill. Housing gravesites that dated back to the late 1800's, it was modernized as any cemetery nowadays would be, with paved roads and neatly manicured rows of headstones set in golf-course grass. Some of Billings' most influential citizens were buried there, with custom grave-toppers that would have been more at home in one of the mojo-heavy graveyards of New Orleans – towering angels, gigantic celtic crosses, and even something that looked like a petrified tree. Mountview's headstone panorama ranged from the banal – the flat in-ground grave markers – to the most eccentric of internment toppings. It would be a perfect place to wander at midnight. Plus, there was no dodging prickly pear cactus.

Jake and I had a tradition in the Montana town in which we both grew up – we'd walk everywhere. It was a different time, in a different world, in a different state, and one could wander all over the city on foot in the dead of night with nothing but the street lamps and a few owls staring back at you. In the Summertime, we'd be joined by a few friends on this endeavor, and we'd all take turns holding a half gallon of ice cream that with four spoons, we'd all dip into while strolling. The Fall excursions were not as well attended, as the weather wasn't quite as hospitable. Yet we hardcore Nighttime Wanderers were not dissuaded from our trek. We set out on foot for about half a mile, hands buried deep in our pockets against the wind, and on our walk to Mountview, discussed what we hoped to find. The night wind had picked up, and it was a perfectly creepy atmosphere in which to hunt to the dead. Jake and I could not be more excited.

We crested into Mountview, careful not to alert the groundskeeper. Mountview is so large that there is a permanent residence there where the groundskeeper lives, right in the front of the cemetery. (I can just imagine *that* ad for employment: Wanted, Groundskeeper. Room and board included. Must be okay with 2,000 roommates.) The porch light was on, so we made sure to slip into the cemetery on the far side. The best part about Mountview was that it was inadvertently organized by most recent to least recent burials, from east to west. This becomes important when one is dealing in finding spirits who may be at unrest.

Why, you inquire? Well, as our Western society has worn on, we have changed our perception of death, and this change in perception affects how we choose to deal with death in the afterlife. Up until modern medicine could all but control the onset of death, with our life support and projected expiration dates when fighting diseases such as cancer, death was a great mystery. And what do we humans do, when faced with the unknown? We fear it, of course.

In the days before diagnosis, we viewed Death as a specter, often brought in on the tail end of great suffering, plucking the breath from our mouths in order to reap us with its icy sickle. Back in the day, Death was something that could come at any time, and there was no rhyme or reason for it's arrival: The flu, childbirth, plague, and let's not forget the many mysteries such as "consumption" (later to be understood as cancer), seizures, diabetes, stroke – the health hazard list was endless. What we pop pills for today killed us yesterday, and none of it made any sense to those who were on the other end of Death's indiscriminant whip. Thus, turn-of-the-century spirits were often taken by surprise, and that surprise would mean struggle with the acceptance of death, the result being more earth-bound turn-of-the-century spirits who are either still very confused about why no one can see them, or who simply were not ready to go, and are unaware of how much time has passed since their physical body expired.

The interesting juxtaposition about this old school view on death is the flipside of mystery, which is total acceptance. Knowing that Death could come at any time, many folks back in the day simply accepted every day as a blessing, and never expected much of a lifespan. Those folks crossed over very easily.

Though accidents and untimely deaths still happen in modern times, today's mortal illnesses come with some sort of instruction manual – one year to live, six months to live – allowing the sick person some down-shifting time to accept the inevitable. Though I don't know if I'm a fan of the "projected death" medical practice, because I've known plenty of people who have fought well beyond the odds to heal and live long lives to expire from old age, I can say that the resonance left behind in a cemetery is different once the folks passed away after 1950. The only commonality I can find for this is the increase in our medical community's ability to diagnose.

For those wanting to ghost hunt in graveyards, it's important to point out here that many spirits don't actually hang around in a cemetery, as that's not where they died. But hey, I was in my very early twenties, so I didn't know that. I just knew it was a spooky place to wander around in the creepy Fall night. Mostly, in cemeteries, there are trace remnants of the emotionality left behind from those mourning the loss of their loved ones. And in that mourning, one can decode the energy signature of how those around the loved one perceived death, culturally, as either "mystery" (turn of the century deaths) or "prepared" (modern burials).

Jake and I started ghost hunting at the oldest part of the cemetery. Dead leaves crunched beneath our feet and wind whistled through odd shaped headstones to create eerie dust devils of debris. We wandered through the headstones, asking spirits if they were present while reading the epitaphs in the yellow light of our should-have-been-retired flashlight. (I'm pretty sure it was Jake's Grandma's, and probably spent a majority of its life earning its rust in a Johnson-era bomb shelter. But back to the story.) We'd find old family plots adorned with recognizable names that still ran established businesses in our town, and it was fascinating how the epitaphs changed as we walked farther west. Inscriptions on older headstones were far more heartfelt and impressive, even macabre, than their modern counterpart: "May our darling daughter never struggle in vain for breath again, now safe in the arms of God." Once we tripped into the mid twentieth century, full bible verses, heart-breaking farewells and ornate carvings gave way to "Loving Mother".

The night was wearing on and though neither Jake nor I wanted to admit it, the midnight weather was turning sour. The cemetery seemed darker, and though that's exactly the kind of creepy we were looking for, the theory of the "creepy" was much more fun than the pitch-black reality of the situation. We began to notice that it was difficult to read the headstones with the weak flashlight, and that's when it dawned on us that the moon had been snuffed out by thick clouds. And *that's* when the realization hit us: All the wind we'd experienced over the last several hours was heralding a whopper storm that had been blowing in over the Beartooth Mountains. It was the second half of the realization that was the stinger – we were on foot.

For the first time, the catastrophic-looking thunderhead that had been barreling in our direction made itself known as silent flashes of purple lightning caught high within the cloud itself illuminated the body of the monster above. As is typical for Montana storms, the thunderhead was epic, vaulting miles into the sky and eclipsing the entire horizon. Considering Montana is Big Sky Country (because when you look up, the sky is truly just HUGE), this was an indication that the storm was even more enormous. Being veterans of this climate, we realized that since the lightning was silent, it wasn't yet touching the ground close enough for us to hear the thunder. This gave us some time, and instead of being frightened, we were exhilarated. Our very own lightning storm, dead leaves, and a graveyard -- in our young minds, we had hit a paranormal home run.

A new enthusiasm in our sails, we weaved through the graveyard asking spirits to come forward as we mused about how we'd wasted all that time looking for poor old Mr. Losekamp at the college when we'd hit the mother lode of eerie, right here. As our flashlight began to fade even further to a milky eggshell color, the flickering of the oncoming lightning stepped in to briefly light up the entire cemetery, one headstone at a time. All we needed was a vampire and a werewolf, and we'd have a classic Universal Studios creature double feature.

This is a good time to point out that back then I didn't know diddly-squat about the physics of spirituality. So, it didn't occur to me that this titan of a thunderhead contained off-the-charts amounts of EMF (electro magnetic fields), and this EMF was charging the air, making the very atmosphere a "ghost battery pack". Spirits will often draw EMF out of the air as fuel to move objects or to communicate. It also didn't occur to me that the rather steady and sudden battery drain in our flashlight began in the cemetery, and more so as the storm rode in. I just chalked it off to Jake's Grandma's five-thousand-year-old-flashlight probably containing ten-thousand-year-old Double D batteries, rather than the sudden battery drain that occurs when spirits pull energy from the air in order to manifest.

Suddenly, here came that howling tell-tale Montana wind, the stuff that says, "Yep. You're done for." This was the kind of wind that one usually associates with tropical storms, only there was nothing topical about the bitter cold with which we were being flogged. I'm certain Hollywood could learn a thing or two about exfoliation and facial peels from the force of the wind raking glass-like bits of razor-sharp dead leaves against our cheeks. Ghosts be damned -- by this time we were seeking some sort of break from the weather.

We headed for a small hill in the center of the cemetery containing a few trees. To heck with the threat of lightning – we were hoping the trunks would break the outrageous pre-arctic gusts. Jake pulled his collar up and I remember wrapping my arms around myself even tighter to lock out the bitter wind. The storm came up faster than we anticipated, with thunder now rumbling just off the periphery. We made the decision to wait it out under the trees in case it started to rain, and while under the trees, to find an abnormally large headstone to huddle behind, using it as a wind break. It certainly wasn't the first time that either one of us had been caught outside in the full-on wrath of a Montana storm. But, it was the first time either one of us had been caught in a storm of this magnitude, after midnight, in a graveyard. And something was starting to feel not right about the entire situation.

I recall the ethers around us changing, and I again attributed this fact to the storm's ability to plummet the barometric pressure. But deep down, I knew that wasn't the case. Storms don't make you feel like you're being watched. The flashlight was now barely sputtering light. It was kind of pathetic. We'd have to hold the flashlight inches from the headstones to make out the deeply carved letters. Finally, the ol' gal gave up with a pithy half-flicker – then complete darkness.

There we were, in the pitch black of midnight, tiny invisible bits of crushed foliage stinging as it pelted against our faces. Thanks to a brilliant flash of lightning, we saw a very large headstone less than ten feet away, closer to the base of the tree. This would make a windbreak on two sides, and a much better place to hunker down and wait out the storm. I grabbed a hold of Jake in the relentless wind and we both stumbled against the weather to stand in the shelter of the towering headstone.

Instantly, the wind was cut by the monolithic grave marker, several feet wide and taller than both of us. We both let out a breath, realizing we'd been holding ours to keep out the whipping dirt. The huge headstone was a few feet up the hill from us, and looked more like a small wall. The wind whistled over the top of the granite and over our heads. We both should have been grateful, yet something seemed wrong. It seemed very wrong, standing in this dead spot. It was too calm, as if we had stepped into a bubble, the weather raging on either side of us.

The lightning flickered several times in a row, allowing the monolithic headstone to be illuminated through the shadows of the tree above. Instead of lettering, what appeared to be carved into the granite were strange characters – deep slashes and strange shapes that looked like ancient Sumerian writing, or runes, rather than any inscription in English. It seemed bizarre, and forced, as if it was supposed to look confusing. It was very out of place, and we both fell silent. The hair on the back of my neck stood up, and it wasn't from the cold. I knew Jake well enough to suspect that from his silence, he had seen what I had seen.

"Could you read that headstone?" I hollered to him above the howling wind.

"No, it's just a bunch of slashes," he answered, trying to sound calm.

"Do you think it's a language?" I inquired again, hoping he'd be familiar with something that I wasn't, because not only had Jake taken Latin in high school, but his family was Jehovah's Witness, and they often studied the translation of ancient languages.

"I don't know…" he trailed off. This was a very bad sign.

I was beginning to feel like a raccoon who realized its paw was caught in an invisible trap. Once an inviting relief from the weather, I could sense a consciousness in this towering black stone mass in front of us, and it leered at us in the dark. Suddenly, a sustained flash of lightning blew up the sky in a blinding white blast, and the huge headstone lit up. Across its granite face, in the place of the strange markings, were deep and unmistakably large letters, spelling the name:

LOSEKAMP

A loud clap of thunder punctuated the drop of both our jaws, as if on cue, and the headstone fell black as the thunder rolled across the sky. I couldn't believe what I was looking at, and Jake's silence tipped me off that he couldn't believe what he was looking at, either. In all of the places, of all of the headstones, in all of the cemeteries in Billings – we finally found Mr. Losekamp.

"No way," I uttered. Jake said nothing.

I then started prattling on and on, a mile a minute, about how we were probably standing on the whole Losekamp family, how disrespectful that was, how wild it was that we found the family plot, on and on and on, and I suddenly felt Jake grab my arm – hard. In fact, it hurt, his fingers curling into my forearm, and that just wasn't like him. I could only make out his silhouette, though he was right next to me, and his silhouette felt panicked. The explosive lightning blew the sky white again, and I could see Jake, his eyes widened in fear, mouth gaping open, his other hand up to his throat, gesturing wildly. His chest heaved yet not a peep came from his mouth and his face was red.

BOOM went the thunder overhead, and Jake fell again into blackness, his silhouette taking off down the hill into the wind, to stand in the open on the paved driving area below. I took off after him, the weather blasting against me. Once away from the shadow of the gravestone, he began to cough furiously. He clutched his chest, coughing. He continued to cough and cough, his back to the wind.

"Are you okay?" I asked frantically. "What happened?"

"It was choking me. I couldn't breathe," he answered hoarsely, barely understandable over the screaming wind as he hacked and coughed between words. "I had to get out of there."

At that moment, I knew we had to get out of that cemetery, period. My worries that something was very wrong were confirmed. Jake was not one who put on a show, or panicked, especially in the face of things that went bump in the night. In fact, he had a constitution of steel. We often joked that he'd make an excellent surgeon, or hitman. Yet here he was, making the choice to flee the scene, and I was right behind him. The ethers were charged with something other than ions and I could feel a swirling all around us that had nothing to do with the wind.

Any fears of the mega storm took a backseat to the paranormal attack. Jake and I bolted in a brisk walk to the edge of the cemetery, staying to the paved road. He continued to cough, and tears ran down his cheeks – not tears of fear, but the physiological kind -- the kind of tears that form when a person can't stop choking. Jake continued to keep his hand over his chest. Though he had great difficulty speaking, he complained that the upper part of his chest was frozen from the inside out. He described the feeling as very painful, like a brain freeze, only in his bronchial tubes. "It felt like a cold claw reached down my throat," he said. "It burns."

The storm raged on as we quickly made our way through the maze of roadways inside of Mountview, this time purposefully crossing right in front of the once-avoided caretaker's house to take advantage of the porch light's illumination. Jake and I burst from the cemetery onto the welcome city sidewalk. Once standing beneath the street light, there was a sense of relief that beset the both of us. One monster down, one more to go -- only ten more blocks on foot and we'd be out of the blowing storm, which was starting to spit frigid rain.

With Mountview Cemetery at our back, we shot up the street. Jake's windpipe finally began to clear. We chatted about what had happened, and how quickly the paranormal ambush had come on. We compared notes about how in the heck a tombstone that clearly read "Losekamp" had moments before looked like some sort of ancient druid etchings from the wrong side of a dark magic ritual. None of it made sense, and none of it involved Casper the Friendly Ghost answering our inane questions.

As we continued up the sidewalk, the light rain whipping sideways, I once again began to feel uneasy. I noticed a twinge of something at back. Though the cemetery was now over two blocks straight behind us, I could feel something coming. It was heading from the cemetery -- straight up the sidewalk. I didn't want to say anything to Jake, as we just cleared up the fact that we wouldn't be going back to Mountview to ghost hunt. But this thing at my back was unnerving, and barreling closer and closer. I stopped talking as I focused on what was coming, and oddly, I noticed that Jake, too, had stopped talking. Then I noticed we had both stopped walking.

I turned to him. "I'm going to say a prayer --"

"Yes," he said urgently, barely letting me finish the word. Jake knew something terrible was coming, too. He felt it, just like I did.

I glanced down the sidewalk and though I could see nothing with the naked eye, my third eye instantly recognized what was bearing down on us: From only the waist up, here came a hideous translucent figure of an older woman from the turn of the century wearing a cream colored high-necked dress with pearl buttons, her hair rolled up in the popular Gibson style. Her mouth gaped inhumanly wide in fury and her pointed facial features stretched in awkward ways as she twisted her neck from side to side as if trying to slither out of her own skin. While hurling toward us, her gnarled hands clawed wildly through the air in front of her as if it would get her to us faster. Upon seeing her curled fingers I recalled what Jake had said, about feeling of a cold claw down his throat – and here it was. The woman's eyes were pale white where the color once lived, and the amount of rage and hatred that exploded out of this entity was palpable, even blocks away. Then I heard in my head a sandpaper voice:

"Loooosekaaaaamp."

Was it Mrs. Losekamp, sprung from the grave, seeking her vengeance for our disrespect to her family's suffering? I said nothing but immediately grabbed Jake's hands. Bowing our heads, we said the Lord's Prayer.

I could feel this thing closing in and I began to pray faster and faster. I noticed that Jake was doing the same thing, and as she approached, he squeezed my hands. I knew he felt this hideous thing coming as well. The ghostly woman neared and I could now hear her shrieking in my head. Even writing this, the recollection of that shrill and ragged sound, full of such pure repulsion, is the thing true nightmares are made of. She was upon us, flying at high speed, and while my physical eyes were closed in prayer I could clearly see in my mind's eye her approach. This ghoul, not ten feet away, made one final thrust with both boney hands as if to run her long and dirty nails through the sides of our heads. The nails were yellow and split, as if she had clawed her way out of her own grave. I did not dare open my eyes with this terrifying banshee upon us.

Suddenly, SPLAT – she seemed to hit an invisible wall a mere three feet from where Jake and I were praying – disappearing instantly into to thin air.

The atmosphere went still except for the rain and rolling thunder.

I didn't say a word to Jake about what I'd just witnessed. But I didn't need to. The moment this hideous creature ran head-on into the spiritual wall of protection that was around us, I noticed Jake's energy changed, and he exhaled, as if, in his mind's eye – he had just witnessed what I had. We stopped praying.

I started to talk. "Did you notice –"

"-- that crazy woman flying up the sidewalk? Yes." He answered.

The ghoul had made itself known to the both of us. We compared a few notes, and he, too, had seen the exact same woman I had, right down to her shrieking mouth, dress, hair, and demonic manicure. I remember being blown away that we had both "seen" the same thing, yet neither of us had used our eyes to do so. That was my first lesson in Psychic Psight.

Oddly – or not so oddly, depending on how you look at it -- our walk home took us right next to a Kingdom Hall, which is a church for the Jehovah's Witnesses. We decided to be on the safe side, lest another one of these things come flying around the corner, and we walked up and touched the door for good measure. I wasn't a Jehovah's Witness but I figured God is God, and this was a house of God, so that was good enough for me, with the way our night was going. We stayed under the church awning until the rain lightened, along with our moods, and then continued to Jake's house, where we promptly dried off, and I headed home.

On my drive home, I checked my rearview mirror obsessively, as I could not get that woman's horrific facial expression out of my mind. I was sure I'd find her leering at me from my backseat through those dead, milky eyes. I finally shook her from my thoughts long enough to reflect on what had occurred. Even though I was extremely inexperienced in the paranormal, it was painfully apparent to me that what we had been dealing with was in no way the ghost of a human, let alone Mrs. Losekamp. In fact, the wretched ghoul was something much worse, a banshee wearing a person suit, and specifically, wearing the suit of a person whom we had been seeking all night.

When I thought about it, I realized we had not been attacked, but rather, we'd brought the night's events on ourselves. We wandered into a graveyard seeking to be terrified. And though the Losekamps were nowhere to be found, and thankfully so, for their sakes, something else -- something awful -- was waiting right there in the wings, happy to pinch hit, lurking in the dark for its chance to dive in and bring us exactly what we were looking for: utter terror.

I've never returned to Mountview to find the Losekamp family plot under the tree…if it's even there. Perhaps it, too, was a specter. That cold Montana Fall of 1991 was my first, and hardest, lesson in ghost hunting: If you seek it, it will find you.

So be careful what you look for.

# 2
# MY NEIGHBOR THE MENTAL HOSPITAL
## WHERE: WESTERN STATE HOSPITAL
## LOCATION: LAKEWOOD, WA

When I was a small child my dad was in the Army. He was in mental health and amongst other things, counseled servicemen who had returned from Vietnam. When I was quite young we traveled a lot as my dad settled into the military. We left from Billings, Montana and lived in Illinois then San Antonio as the Army moved my dad from the graduate program at the University of Chicago to a base in Texas. San Antonio had some huge cockroaches and the heat was ridiculous. While I was there I rode my tricycle into the pool. Hey, I was three, and I'm assuming that it seemed like a good idea. I don't recall doing this, but I'm told I had the good sense to hold my breath as I sat on the bottom of the pool, still hanging onto my tricycle, just looking around at the big blue world I'd plunged into.

My dad dived in and pulled me out. From that point forward, I was doomed to wear bright orange floaties on my arms to keep me above the water. Having been below in its quiet depths, above seemed very anticlimactic. That part I do recall.

As a family we eventually dived north to the Pacific Northwest where my dad was stationed at Fort Lewis in Tacoma, WA. We lived in a very modest apartment in the town of Lakewood. We would stay put there for several years. I attended school all the way through third grade while in Lakewood. At that point in my life – it was a sedentary record.

Lakewood was an eerie place caught in the crosshairs of some really awful geomagnetic activity and some really awful history. Right next to

Lakewood was Steilacoom, a township named after the Steilacoom Indians who lived on Chambers Bay. Besides the fact that Steilacoom is haunted as can be, most of which being related to the deceased Native Americans who lost the fight over the hill at Fort Steilacoom, the town itself has some very unsettling geomagnetic properties beneath it's feet. Steilacoom is a beautiful waterfront town, but like Amityville, New York, it's a paranormal magnet for yuck. Lakewood, its land-locked lake-filled neighbor whose northern border was the Vortex of Chamber's Creek Canyon, was worse. As such, the United States Military was drawn to build a fort there. Amazing how that trend seems to repeat itself throughout history.

Fort Steilacoom was a huge player in the settling of the Washington Territory, built in 1849 to quell the local Indian uprisings. During its reign, Fort Steilacoom housed a number of captives such as Chief Leschi of the Nisqually Indian Tribe. Considered a dangerous insurgent, an attempt was made on Chief Leschi's life by the Washington Territorial Governor, Isaac Stevens. Since Governor Stevens was a better bureaucrat than assassin, he failed, so they slapped poor Chief Leschi in Fort Steilacoom's brig. His crime? Surviving the hit on his life. The fact was, Chief Leschi and his Nisqually Nation were simply casualties in the fight against the conscienceless Western Expansion.

In a twist of irony, it was not actually the military that wanted to do away with the chief, but the business interests in the private sector. To justify his stay in the brig, the private sector trumped up murder charges *against* poor Chief Leschi and tied them to a former Indian raid on the fort. Though Lieutenant August Kautz presented solid evidence at the trial proving that Chief Leschi was not even present at the raid in question, the chief was declared guilty and sentenced to death. The fort's officers were not happy with this unjust verdict. Already on shaky ground with local Native American tribes, the last thing they needed was blood on their hands from a third party's political war. Agenda-driven territorial government officials clashed with the fort's officers as to how to proceed with carrying out Chief Leschi's unfortunate sentence. A disgusted Lt. Col. Casey demanded that the innocent chief be executed at least 300 yards from Fort Steilacoom and that the military remain uninvolved. Chief Leschi met his end, hanged from an oak tree by civil authorities rather than regular Army troops. It was 146 years later that Chief Leschi was pardoned of his "crime". On December 10, 2004, an historical court led by Washington State Supreme Court Chief Justice Gerry Alexander unanimously exonerated him.

Fort Steilacoom closed its doors in 1868.

Now, on the corner of Steilacoom Boulevard and 83rd Avenue SW in Lakewood, WA, the Oakbrook Shopping Center looms large. Next to the parking lot, encircled with sidewalks, a granite rock stands awkward in a small grass plot beneath an oak in front of the Dollar Tree. It reads:

*Leschi*
*Chief of the Nisquallies*
*Martyr to the vengeance*
*of the unforgiving white man*
*was hanged*
*300 yards S.E. from here*
*February 19, 1858*

*Erected 1963 by Pierce County*
*Pioneer & Historical Assn.*

And what became of Fort Steilacoom, the military installment built over the top of hot geomagnetic ley lines? Well it's now Western State Hospital, of course – the largest mental institution not only on the west coast, but west of the Mississippi River. The land was bruised by the twisted geomagnetic veins beneath, and on the bruise was built a fort. The bruise was then bloodied, and on the blood was built a mental institution. Because that's how white people recycle.

Western State is still in operation, though its doors were closed in 1875 due to heinous neglect and severe abuse of patients back when it was Fort Steilacoom Asylum, predating Washington's statehood by almost 20 years.

As most turn-of-the-century asylums, Western State Hospital was accustomed to horror in its hallways. In 1915, a bill was introduced in Washington State that would result in the sterilization of every patient in the Washington mental hospital and institution system. If authorities felt an individual would "produce children with an inherited tendency to crime, insanity, feeble-mindedness, idiocy, or imbecility, and there is no probability that the condition of such person will improve to such an extent as to render procreation by such person advisable[1]" the patients would not be released until sterilized. The law went live in 1921, and 685 people were sterilized statewide -- 501 women and 148 men. Nearly 75%

---

[1] W. C. Rucker, 1915 - "More 'Eugenic Laws'" *The Journal of Heredity* vol. VI, pp. 219-226

of these patients were women, with one African American woman being sterilized twice – once at the age of 15 and upon failed tied tubes resulting in pregnancy, again at 19 with an abortion and full hysterectomy. Of course, most of these "humane sterilizations" were executed on either the mentally ill -- 256 women and 147 men -- or on the mentally underdeveloped, with 243 women and 33 men being put through the humiliation. Just to be thorough, a few rapists and habitual criminals were also sterilized in Washington State, along with epileptics, "moral degenerates", and gays, before the barbaric law was repealed in 1942, deemed as unconstitutional.

Gee – ya think?

In 1944, Western State Hospital was home to famed Seattle-born actress Francis Farmer, who suffered from horrendous bouts with mental illness that eventually ruined her life and career. Following the Hollywood star to her new home in 1949, the *Seattle Post-Intelligencer* exposed the dismal treatment of the patients by an incredibly understaffed medical team. Frontal lobotomies and electro-shock treatment were common, along with insulin therapy – a process where a patient was overdosed with insulin to inspire "mentally cleansing" after experiencing convulsions and coma. The newspaper went on to report more than 2,700 patients were piled like rotting lumber into the historic and decaying wards ~ 500 over capacity. In 1947, a fire broke out in the crumbling buildings resulting in the death of two patients.

It's never a good idea to build a house of pain on already wounded land.

Yet the land would continue to swallow the pain. As it was with all mental hospitals of the day, the cemetery was a place of secrecy and disgrace. Still looming high on the old Hill Ward farm grounds, the name given to the dormitory up on the hill that housed the patients who worked on the hospital's farm, the Western State Hospital Cemetery contains 3,200 people, all patients between 1876 and 1953. Small, flat stone markers are sunken into the ground bearing not names of those who are interned but numbers on small bronze plaques, now blackened with age. The mentally ill were considered such pariahs that as a measure of privacy for the family members left behind, no patient's name would be placed on the grave markers. Sterilized and abandoned, these human beings were stripped of even their name come death.

Today, those graves remain -- right next to a dog park and a small lake, in the middle of Fort Steilacoom Park. I know. As a young child, I ran across the tops of the graves there, playing Frisbee with my parents. We lived about one mile, if that, down the road from Western State

Hospital on 83rd Ave SW in Lakewood. Back then, in the 1970's, the graves were neglected to the point of being nearly invisible, mashed deep into the overgrown grass. There was no additional signage indicating that forgotten human beings were buried there. Picnickers spread blankets over the graves, occasionally tugging at the shaggy grass and curiously pondering the very small plaques containing numbers. Guesses would fly, from old latitude and longitude markers left over from the Army's occupation of the land to contractor's markers. No one knew that within the large open field over which Pippin look-alikes in their Richard Simmons curls flew kites with rainbow tails, 3,200 bodies lay beneath.

Finally, on March 14th of 2009, society grew a conscience and dedicated the Hill Ward Memorial, complete with official signage, indicating presence of the people buried there. The memorial is a haunting and beautiful work, handling the sensitive issue of remembering the trauma that occurred on that very land -- brutal wars with the Native Americans, the slaughtering of settlers, and the inhumane and barbaric practices of early psychiatric medicine – while wrapping the concept in reverent hope for a better future. Built into the ground and including some of the original ruins of the Hill Ward Dormitory, which was closed in 1965, visitors walk through a labyrinth whose stones mark important historical dates and times. It's an eerie and complicated dedication for an eerie and complicated place.

As a child, I remember thinking that the entire area was incredibly melancholy. Goosebumps would erupt on my arm in the blazing summer heat as the oppressive EMF (Electro Magnetic Fields) would drape even the most upbeat Marsha Brady wanna-be in a cloak of oppression. I never liked the way it felt there. But since it was close to the house my family often went to that park. When you're a kid you're just happy to go outside and play with your young, hip parents, even if it is over the top of invisible graves next to an abandoned insane asylum. I began to look at the place like a haunted house amusement park complete with ghosts, though I didn't really think about spirits in such a concrete way at that age. I just knew that the place contained very unhappy people that I couldn't see. My closest foray with ghosts was Scooby Doo, and much to my dismay every Saturday morning, the "ghosts" just turned out to be disingenuous land developers and cranky old men -- who would have gotten away with it, too, if it wasn't for those meddling kids.

Unlike Scooby Doo, which could never hold the creepy feel though an entire episode, the entire Lakewood area couldn't shake the creepy feel for even one day. A bizarre mixture of Human and Elemental spirits (who migrated up from the vortex known as Chambers Creek) were involved in active and residual hauntings, all while snared in the straining geomagnetic ley lines like flies trapped against a paranormal spider's web. To add to the overtly-macabre that was Fort Steilacoom Park, the old abandoned asylum dormitory was still standing right by the edge of the cemetery. May I just take a moment to point out that the city of Lakewood decided it was a good idea to deem this location a "park"?

Thank you. Onward.

As all incredibly haunted locations, the Hill Ward dormitory would beg a person to come in, staring blankly into one's soul with its windowless, black eyes. My parents and I would relent to the call of the tomb and climb in through the open doorways. In the 1970's no one yet believed in safety or locking off dangerous spaces. Back then, it pretty much was a given that if you were stupid enough to get crushed, killed, or infected with typhus, that was your own problem. Not believing in saving anyone from themselves, the dead building had been left wide-open by the city of Lakewood, abandoned for a little over ten years. Ashen concrete walls were the color of a corpse and had not yet been desecrated with the colorful graffiti that would later define its ruins. The ghost of Hill Ward stood towering over the park, an ominous reminder that suffering paved the way for picnics.

Walking through this vacant monstrosity was an exercise in keeping a level head and tempting the hygiene fates. A skeleton of a once mighty tyrant, the old mental asylum still smelled of human waste. Padded rooms dotted the first floor and upon standing in one of these mildew-riddled pockets of despair, I wouldn't last but a few seconds. Not only was the smell of rotting cotton batting more than a person could take, but the energy of fear, dread, and damnation still hung thick in the air. And, if you listened, you could actually hear wailing emerge from the batting as it peeled into the room like the spilled guts of an interrogated prisoner.

That's a lot to take in when you're seven.

Old rusted hospital headboards were stacked against the walls and cane-backed wheelchairs leered from the corners, thick with dust. Even in the broad daylight, the place was a frightening testament to the discarded. I remember my folks telling me not to touch anything and not to go upstairs, though I desperately wanted to. The marble staircase had a huge banister which disappeared into the darkness of the floor above. I wanted to rush up those stairs and into the awaiting arms of something deliciously frightening torn right out of the Scooby Doo play book. I was none too happy to be told to stay on the first floor. At seven years of age, I was a professional Asker of Why. In response, my parents mentioned the upstairs floor may cave in. I recall thinking this reason was one of those juicy overblown tidbits that parents would concoct simply because they didn't feel like being bothered with the request. I could feel "people" upstairs. They weren't very nice people, but that was the fun of it. I was with my folks, so by my seven year old logic, investigating what was causing the tension I was feeling upstairs would have been a safe endeavor. We never did go up and in hindsight I'm lucky my parents let me crawl through the nasty building in the first place. They were as curious as me. Who wouldn't be? This was the place horror films were made of, and there we were, snooping around. Shaggy and Scooby were going to be *so* jealous.

We were wrapping up our visit, crawling back out one of the doorways, when footsteps sounded in the open room behind us. My dad had cleared the building and my mom was encouraging me to crawl through next. I turned to look into the empty room, the light streaming in through the broken windows, and I could hear someone walking on the broken glass. My mom heard it too, and I could tell she was trying to whisk me through the semi-blocked doorway quickly without tipping me off that she was freaked out by the disembodied footsteps as well. In the tense, quiet pause, I was just crawling through the maze of junk blocking the door when several rusted headboards at the end of the room suddenly slammed themselves to the floor as if shoved with great force. The impact and the crashing sound were both incredibly out of place. Those headboards were practically rusted to one another in the Washington State humidity, so the likelihood of them "falling over" was less than zero.

Someone was tired of our intrusion.

My mom shot out of there like a cork coming out of Red Rider's air rifle. That was the end of our Hill Ward Dormitory investigations. I no longer cared what was upstairs. If those invisible people were tossing around iron headboards, I was out. That kind of agitation just wasn't normal.

Nothing about living in Lakewood was normal. As a little kid I would walk to what was then the Thunderbird Shopping Center in search of Lemon Heads and a Marathon candy bar. When I'd get there, I'd climb the "monument" to Chief Leschi in its former 1970's incarnation – a much less grand rock sitting next to a garbage can, slapped with an oxidized copper plaque. I had no idea what it said. Often, an abandoned soda can was sitting on top on the stone, which I always found odd since the garbage was right there. In the 1970's, cultural neglect seemed to be a way of life.

Lakewood was just not a happy place. The energy there was all wrong. No matter how hard I tried as a child, I never felt safe while living there. I didn't fear people, but something else, a resonance that came out of the ground. I felt as though at any minute the earth would open a giant drain and everything on the surface would be sucked in. Lakewood felt like it was just a tad out of phase with the rest of reality – like the looks-normal-but-isn't dimension in *Jacob's Ladder*. The ground felt as though it were constantly seething, just rigidly angry that anyone dwelled above. I came to find out later that the land on which our apartment building sat was the area where countless settlers were slain in Indian attacks and countless Native Americans were killed by the cavalry during raids on the fort. To make matters worse in this spiritually unstable environment, while we lived in that apartment building, my infant brother passed away from Sudden Infant Death Syndrome. It was traumatic. Yet even as a child of five years old, I processed the event as just the type of thing I would expect to happen there. Again, the place never felt safe. Perhaps I was picking up on not only the active spirit life, but the residual haunting of the anxieties of settlers attacked in the night or the wary fear of Native Americans ambushed by the cavalry. We were living on a battlefield and likely, a graveyard. Perhaps I was also picking up on the outrageous amount of Elementals running amok thanks to the Vortex of Chambers Creek Canyon, just north. Or perhaps I was even picking up the large amount of Off-Worlder (ET) activity that was taking place in the woods outside of Steilacoom by Fort Lewis. Lakewood was an EMF cesspool, and I honestly expected the land would eat us all before it was said and done. In a way, it did: My brother died, my mom had open heart surgery at Madigan Hospital on Fort Lewis, and my parents ended up getting divorced -- all while living in that apartment.

That place sucked. Literally. It sucked the life force out of everything that touched it.

It even sucked the life out of the plants. Our apartment complex butted against a vacant field. The field had once been the back end of an airstrip in the 1940's but had since grown over with flora and fauna that was typical of the Northwest Prairies except for one thing: Everything in the field was dead but the scotch broom. It's hard to believe that any plant life would die in the Pacific Northwest considering the climate is deemed a temperate rain forest. If there's one thing the Northwest has, it's rain. Lots and lots and lots of rain. So the dead plant life in this enormous field always stood out. The grass was dead and any Gerry Oaks that once stood were dead. In fact, the trees were not only dead, but fallen over and blanched grey, as if every bit of what the tree had to offer had been drained by Hardwood Vampires. There was only one lone tree left standing in the field, its gnarled branches raised high, frozen in defiance against its own death. The carcass of the tree was frightening, and seemed as though at any moment its limbs would come alive and snatch one of us off the ground in its brittle branchy fist. The tree should have starred in a Tim Burton film.

Every time I looked at the tree, I thought to myself: "People were hung here." I thought "hung" and not "hanged" because I was seven, and didn't know any better. Even so, it was just something that the tree's cadaver was energetically stamped with – hanging. The thick branch where I could sense the hanging had taken place had been sawn off at some point, leaving a grey, barren stump high above. Keep in mind that the process of slipping a noose around someone's neck and hanging them wasn't something that was on the top of my awareness at seven years old. There was no internet and television was different then. Though I was born in Montana, we had been traveling since I was two and I'd not yet been exposed to the whole "Old West" mentality. I did, however, know exactly what a hanging was, and how it happened – mostly thanks to the tree. Several men had been hanged on that tree. It seemed to be that most of them were bad guys, misbehaving military, and a small few whose crime was being Native American. Again, the area was right by Fort Steilacoom so it made sense that a good hanging tree would be close by. Just to put any curious minds at rest – this was not the tree from which Chief Leschi was hanged. Its once-mighty branches choked the life out of much lower profile offenders.

Down the center of the tree was the scar from the blow that brought its death -- an enormous burn mark. The tree had been hit by lightning and I'm sure died from the impact. Now would be the time to point out that for all the rain in Western Washington, the climate hardly ever supported lightning when storms rolled in. And now would also be the time to point out how creepy it was that a hanging tree was struck by lightning.

Huh. Maybe it *was* the tree where poor innocent Chief Leschi was hanged?

The burned-out hanging tree reigned supreme over the raggedy field which stretched about a block until meeting up with Western State Hospital -- easily visible across the expanse. I would stand in the field and stare at the old buildings that made up the hospital complex in the distance. I could feel the hundreds of heads exploding, hazy, lost in their own nightmares while wide awake, spun out on their own chaos between space and time. Maybe Lakewood had adopted their energy signature. Or maybe these poor mentally ill souls were trapped on this hideous land already vibrating with discontent, as some sort of living hell. I actually recall thinking at seven years old that I was amazed they chose to erect a mental hospital where the feeling of uneasiness was so present. It seemed very cruel to me.

The vacant field was typical of the 1970's. Rusted bones of cars were overgrown with scotch broom, abandoned shopping carts lay on their side, and dead garden hoses hid snake-like in the weeds. I played with a great group of kids from the apartment complex and we would sneak off into the field to build forts from the Mad Max refuse that had been discarded there. We weren't supposed to be playing out there because anything could have happened to us and not one parent would have been the wiser. The 1970's were infamous for the outbreak in kidnappings, and that fear became a way of life in every child's home. Yet we were kids, and the only thing that eclipsed the idea of being kidnapped by creepy strangers was sneaking off and playing in a creepy field.

Usually, even when we'd play in the field, we'd stick to the side of the field that touched the apartment complex. But once in awhile we'd become very brave and wander closer into the center where the scotch broom was higher and the bounty of weird junk through which to comb and build was less picked over. One afternoon the gang managed to make a fort using the door from a car, an old hollowed log, and a piece of tarp that was found wadded up somewhere. The tarp had string attached so we really were living large with a tent-like structure. This became our base for the next week. Every day we'd go out to the field and try and find the fort – because of course, we made sure it was hard to find to discourage other would-be child-truders. Once the secret fort was located, we'd scour the field for more treasures to add to our End Times architecture. In all the time we lived in Lakewood, this was the best fort that my little gang had ever constructed. And that was saying something considering many of the forts were built within the middle-earth wrapping of blackberry bushes, and you couldn't beat those for privacy. The downside of the blackberry bush forts was not their barbs and brambles, but the fat, hairy, and humongous northwest spiders.

I could deal with the Dead. I could deal with the Elementals. I could deal with the oppressive EMF and the Bodies and the ET's and the Kidnappers. But I drew the line at spiders.

I still do.

It was during one of these afternoons playing in the fort that we looked up to see the scotch broom rustling in the distance. Now, scotch broom is really tall and if you're a child, it's extra tall. So whatever was causing this scotch broom to rattle back and forth was rather large and cutting its way through the forest of weeds like an ocean liner slipping through the Atlantic. I caught the attention of my other little pals, alerting them that we had some "incoming". We all hunkered down behind the log, peering out from beneath the droopy construction tarp, waiting to see what would spill out in the patchy clearing before us. Would it be a dog? A wild boar? A crazed robot doing the dastardly will of an evil genius? Our first-grade minds ran wild. As the rustling approached, we fell silent.

Out from the spit-bug infested scotch broom burst a confused man who must have been in his 40's. His limp brown hair was greasy and his bangs were cut too short. He was crying. Whining to himself, he whimpered, looking from one side to the other then up to the sky as if desperately seeking something. With his hands extended, he groped the air as if at any minute he'd find some mystical tow rope to pull him back on course. On his feet were a pair of filthy white slippers and he had a few small cuts bloodied on his shins. The man wore a hospital gown that was loosely tied in the back. His bare rump occasionally winked from between the flapping edges of the cloth. The gown was a familiar give-away: He was a patient from across the field at Western State Hospital who had wandered off, now utterly lost.

We all hit the deck behind the log, holding our breath and praying he wouldn't come in our direction.

This wasn't the first time we'd witnessed lost patients wandering the field. Though it didn't happen very often, Western State would lose one or two of its finest, and they'd awkwardly make their way across the field in a sobbing frenzy like a premenstrual zombie. The last one to wander past was a woman who was well into her 70's, patches of her thin white hair completely gone around the crown of her head, and her teeth still back in the jar at Western State. As an adult, I would not hesitate to dive in and help these poor individuals. But as a child that wasn't an option. We weren't supposed to be in the field in the first place. Add a potentially dangerous mentally ill stranger to the mix and that was sure to net a spanking of Spartan proportion for any child, back in the day.

The disoriented man shuffled in a large circle in front of us, crying and making vocalizations that sounded like a wounded animal. Even as young as I was, I could tell that the man was developmentally delayed.

The worst part was that I could feel him – he was so incredibly scared. I couldn't believe that this poor man had to deal not only with his own disorientation, but the wretched energy of the field itself. I felt very badly for him but at the same time, I was afraid of the blinding chaos I could see in his head, so I kept my white-blonde towhead smartly ducked behind the log.

The man didn't seem to notice our fort right in front of him – likely because it looked like a pile of trash to the untrained eye. So he continued his desperate stomping and flailing, crying as he crashed through the scotch broom. We all lay on our backs in the dirt for a while, watching the black tarp flap above in the breeze while one or the other of us peaked up to see if the coast was clear. The man was making such a racket that at the very least we could track him as he wandered away. As scary as the encounter was, adventures like this were exactly why we played in the field.

That once-vacant field is still dominated by kids. This time, instead of sneaking out of the neighboring apartment complex, the kids are housed at The Child Study and Treatment Center built where the once-towering hanging tree stood tall. Known as CLIP, it's the most intensive inpatient psychiatric treatment program available for Washington State residents between the ages of 5 and 18.

The land was bruised by the twisted geomagnetic veins beneath, and on the bruise was built a fort. The bruise was then bloodied, and on the blood was built a mental institution.

Because that's how white people recycle.

# 3
# OUR HOMEMADE OUIJA BOARD
## WHERE: GRANNY AND GRANDPA'S BASEMENT
## LOCATION: HARDIN, MONTANA

Let it be known that I think Ouija Boards are dangerous. I really do. I think they're dangerous because you just don't know who you are getting on the other end. Good spirits don't need to talk to someone by tapping that person's energy and moving a planchette across a board. That's just not the attention positive spirits seek. Negative spirits aren't stupid, and they know that if they represent as a creepy crawly, most folks won't want to play anymore. So of course, the negative spirit is going to pretend to be some sweet little thing to keep the attention of the person talking with it, until all hell breaks loose and someone is pinned down in the middle of the night because the creepy spirit has drawn enough power from the individual to terrorize them in their own home. Think of Ouija Boards like the hole in the wall that lets in mice. It just shouldn't be there.

Of course, you couldn't have told me any of this when I was fourteen. In fact, that there's not much you can tell a fourteen year old girl that she'll listen to except, "Hey, the phone's for you." So when my cousin's best friend explained to me what a Ouija Board was and suggested we try it – I was in.

When I was fourteen years old, I had the extreme pleasure of getting the chance to spend an entire month at my grandparents' house in Hardin, Montana, with my best friend "Pearl", my cousin "Tracy", and her best friend "Liz". Pearl and I were inseparable and so were Tracy and Liz, so my Granny, in her wisdom, suggested we all go stay together.

I'm not sure if my Granny had a death wish or if she just enjoyed a challenge, but she and my Grandpa took in four fourteen-year-old girls for the summer, and loved it. My grandparents were extraordinary people and as an adult, I'm even more aware of how selfless they were with us grandkids.

Hardin, at the time, was a town of about 1,500 people, and it's exactly what you'd think of when you picture the town in *It's a Wonderful Life*. It had one street that ran up the center of town, aptly named Main Street, that was dotted with brick buildings erected in the early 1900's, one bank, and one grocery store – Safeway. Hardin was a stone's throw away from the Crow Indian Reservation and many of its residents were Crow. However, the largest demographic in Hardin was actually grasshoppers. Hardin sat in the middle of miles and miles of tall rolling grass on any given side, and it's amazing that garter snakes weren't in higher occupancy.

My grandparents had this fantastic house that my Grandpa had designed and it was unlike anything I'd ever seen. Not only that, it was unlike anything Hardin had ever seen. It was Jetson's Chic with its tilted roof and high triangular windows. The front of the house was a wall of stone, and the back of the house was a floor-to-ceiling wall of windows that looked into the back yard. This house was all about privacy. It had a gigantic brick fireplace island, painted white, that divided the living room from the dining room, and the fireplace was open on both sides. The home was extremely progressive for its time, and was carpeted with thick shag that was cream with occasional flecks of olive. I wish the house was still in the family. It was truly unique.

Pearl and I shared a bedroom and Tracy and Liz shared the other bedroom. We got into all sorts of harmless mischief that summer, where the high Montana desert heat would bake the day to around 115 degrees. To get out of the blazing oven, we'd all congregate in the basement, which was decorated to be rather trendy in that 1979 sort of way with rusts, avocados and blacks.

The basement had the classic arsenal for the social-drinking *Bewitched* generation of the early 1960's – a wet bar, some squishy couches, an 8 track tape player, and of course, another fireplace. We were listening to a warped Neil Diamond yodel out "Rambling Rose" when Liz brought up Ouija Boards. I'd never heard of such a thing, a board with the alphabet that a spirit could use to spell out words. My cousin Tracy thought I was kidding, as she and Liz had played with a Ouija Board several times. I was truly naïve in this way, growing up in a traditional Christian household. We no more had a Ouija Board than a collection of Led

Zeppelin albums. I asked Liz how she knew about contacting the dead, and my cousin Tracy changed the subject. Tracy later pulled me aside and told me Liz's sister had committed suicide a month before, and she was working though it any way she could.

Now in hindsight, I'm sure that's why my grandparents let all four of us stay with them that summer – to give Liz a chance to take her mind off of the awful situation at home.

I got to thinking about the prospect of contacting spirits, and it seemed scary but intriguing. My best friend Pearl didn't think it was a good idea to try a Ouija Board, but she was overruled by three other hormonal fourteen-year-olds. Let it be said on record that Pearl was the only one of us with a lick of sense, but she was also the most easy-going of the group, so Ouija Board it was.

Obviously, this was going to have to be a covert action. None of us were going to go ask my Granny, a commanding woman who really should have been the Queen of England, if she had a Ouija Board -- even though Liz assured me it was sold as a board game.

A board game -- can you see that toy development meeting?

*Terry Toymaker:* "Hey, Mattel, I came up with this great idea – it's a board that allows the dead to talk to you!"

*Mattel:* "Cool. How does it work?"

*Terry Toymaker:* "I have no idea!"

*Mattel:* "Cool. How do you know you're talking to a dead **person**?"

*Terry Toymaker:* "You don't!"

*Mattel:* "Cool. Let's sell it to kids."

…Because that makes sense.

Seeing as none of us had the stones to ask my Granny if in her closet under her Yahtzee game, she had some cult board game that contacted spirits, I asked Liz for the specs of the Ouija Board. It seemed easy enough to make – all you needed was an alphabet on one side, some numbers on the other, and a "yes" and "no" area. I cut out little pieces of paper and taped all the numbers and letters in a circle on a Formica table in the basement, as I thought the Formica would be nice and slippery for the planchette to move around upon. And, for the planchette, I borrowed the lid off of the toothpick holder on the bar. I figured it was light plastic, so it would move around easily, too. After all, I was trying to accommodate dead people who had no fingers. I figured lightweight was pretty important.

This cutting and sizing and taping thing was quite a process, and the whole project was soundtracked by my best friend Pearl with her hit, *Guys? I don't think this is a very good idea.*

What could go wrong? It was a homemade Ouija Board. It probably wouldn't even work. Anyway, what self-respecting spirit wanted to talk to four fourteen-year-old girls through a Formica table? For me, it was more about whether or not I could construct this thing. Once I got the make-shift Ouija Board made, we hid it beneath a table cloth – avocado green – so we could start using it the next evening. We all went to sleep that night as if we were preparing for a bank heist, all with cat-ate-the-canary grins—all except Pearl. Who reminded everyone that she thought this was a bad idea.

We waited anxiously throughout the next day, until my grandparents went to sleep, and then changed our clothes into outfits of all-black in order to address the Ouija Board. After all, we *were* doing something spooky, so black seemed to bring some sort of seriousness to the occasion. The black clothing was Liz's idea, and again, in hindsight, poor Liz was trying to work out some pretty heavy stuff within. But, we were fourteen, and Liz's darker leanings were to be eclipsed by the basic fact that in a group of fourteen-year-old girls, all-black was just flat-out cool.

We removed the avocado table cloth to expose our secret Formica Ouija Board, and Tracy and Liz mentioned that we couldn't have any lights on or it wouldn't work. So we drug four candles out of the cupboard and put one on each corner of the table. The candles were typical of the '70s – votive candles in those extremely thick colored glass candle holders. With the light off, the candles lit, and all of us sitting at the table, it was time to begin.

I asked Liz what we were supposed to do. She told us all to place one finger on lid. Pearl made sure to tell everyone that this was a bad idea, one last time. But, under the pressure of three impatient Tweens, Pearl's finger ended up on the lid, too.

Liz led out. "Are there any spirits with us?"

There was no response. Liz asked again, and to my utter surprise, the lid actually moved. It slowly slid over to "yes".

There was an eruption of nervous giggles (consider the crowd). I looked at my cousin Tracy and said, "You pushed that."

"No, I didn't," she blurted earnestly.

"Liz," I kept going, "then you pushed it."

"I don't think this is a good idea," said Pearl.

"I didn't push it," insisted Liz. "That's what happens. The spirits use our energy to move the marker."

I wasn't actually buying it at this point. I was sure that my cousin and her friend were pulling my leg. But I figured I'd gone through all the trouble to make the board, and we were dressed for the occasion, so why not continue.

We asked the Formica Ouija Board another question and the lid moved again, but this time, I noticed that my cousin removed her finger and so did Liz, so Pearl and I were the only ones with our fingers on the lid as it slid to its answer. I looked at Pearl.

"Are you pushing that?" I asked her.

"No, but you must be," she replied.

Well, I knew I wasn't pushing it, and I knew that Pearl wasn't a liar, which meant that we had a real, live spirit on the other line -- which also meant that my Formica Ouija Board worked. I was completely proud of myself, as my art project was actually functional. Now I was really interested in what was going on.

We continued to ask the Formica Ouija Board all sorts of questions. We were going to the state fair the next day in Billings, and we asked the board if we'd meet any boys. (Of course. Always ask those on the other side the important life questions.)

The board responded "yes". Liz asked who would meet a boy, and the board slowly spelled out my name, going to each letter. I was fascinated. Liz was not happy with the answer. I asked the board what color hair the boy would have. The board spelled out "brown". We went through a few more questions, but then the board went quiet. So we decided to go to sleep as we had an early morning the next day to make the drive to Billings which was about 45 minutes away. We blew out the candles, hid the Formica Ouija Board under the avocado table cloth, and turned in.

In the spirit of the evening's theme, we had decided to sleep downstairs in the same room as the Ouija Board that night, pulling the couch cushions onto the floor and making make-shift beds everywhere. We turned out the lights, zipped up our sleeping bags, and nodded off.

That night, I was awakened by a strange sensation – a light and cool breeze running up my legs. Only it was *inside* my zipped sleeping bag. It was enough to wake me, and I was half asleep, so though I had an acute awareness that something was in my sleeping bag with me, it really did seem harmless. In my mind's eye, I saw this thirty-something prairie schoolmarm who was hovering above me, stopping by to check on me. I realized the energy felt familiar, and clocked this spirit as the one who had told me that I was going to meet a boy the next day. There was something a little odd about the whole experience, but I was either too tired or too in denial about how creepy that all was – so I rolled over and went back to sleep.

The next day we went to the fair, and sure enough, out of all of us, I was the only one approached by a boy – who happened to have brown hair. At that point, we were all in awe of the Formica Ouija Board and its talents, and had a list of questions to ask of it, that night when we got home.

Liz was particularly surly that night. She really wanted to meet a boy that day at the fair, and I didn't care whether I met one or not, so she was feeling like the Universe had somehow completely ripped her off. We got into our black clothes, lit the candles, and fired up Old Formica. Liz asked the spirit all sorts of questions about death. The board was answering in some rather disturbing ways, and Pearl mentioned that maybe we shouldn't be talking about that sort of stuff. I was beginning to get a touch icked-out myself about Liz's death obsession, so I lightened up the mood a little by asking the spirit its name.

It slowly spelled "H-E-L", and then hesitated. My stomach was just starting to sink when it quickly completed "E-N". Helen.

"Hello, Helen," said my cousin Tracy.

I was still stuck on the HEL part. As the board spelled HEL, my mind went right to "from hell", and the lid instantly stopped moving, as if it could hear my thoughts. The subsequent "EN" really felt like a ruse.

Something wasn't adding up.

We continued to ask questions about our future, and the board continued to answer, though some of the answers seemed to be getting a little brisk. That, coupled with the whole HEL thing, plus the situation with the sleeping bag the night before, was making me pause. Something wasn't right. I finally broke in and asked the spirit:

"Helen, when were you born?"

The lid barely moved between the "yes" and the "no". It shook a bit, but stayed right in the middle. My stomach continued to sink. I asked again:

"Helen, when did you die?"

Again, the lid reacted the same way – twitching a little, but not moving to either "yes" nor "no". My stomach sank completely. I may have not been paranormally savvy, but I knew no birth and no death meant we weren't dealing with a human being. I was well aware of the concept of Demons, having grown up in a Foursquare Evangelical church. What else would never have been born and never have died? Nowadays, I'd answer that question with "Elemental", "Inter-

Dimensional", or "Angel" as well. But at the time, I went right to Demon, mostly because that's what I was scared we had on the hook.

"Helen," I asked, "What color is your hair?"

The board spelled out B-L-A-C-K. Black. Of course.

I paused at the next question because I didn't want to know the answer. Yet, at the same time, I felt it was important. I put on my big-girl panties and continued.

"Helen," I asked slowly, "what color are your eyes?"

The lid hesitated, and then moved slowly across the board, spelling out R-E-D. ...Red?

Pearl took her hand off the lid. I knew she was done with this exercise in the mystical. I was, too.

I immediately went into Rebuke-a-Demon mode, with the get-thee-behind-me-Satans and all. Liz became very angry, and said that she didn't want me to chase off the spirit because she hadn't asked about her sister yet. Tracy and Pearl sat dumbfounded. I told her that it wasn't a spirit, it was a Demon, and we couldn't talk to it any further. Poor Liz started to cry out of frustration and I kept up my Demon-rebuking at full tilt until -- BANG -- one of the thick glass candle votives, the one to my right elbow, popped in half, like someone had hit it with an axe and split the glass straight down the middle. The two halves of glass fell to the table. I noticed that it had not broken at its seam.

The other girls stared in disbelief.

This was a very thick votive, and had been around for years. The candle's flame was nowhere close to the votive walls, so clearly, it wasn't the heat that caused the break. Yet there it lay, in two pieces.

I was scared out of my wits and had no idea what was happening, but figured that we must have had a Demon on the line, otherwise why would it react so strongly to prayer? I'd now recognize this menace as a low-level dark spirit who was full-on messing with us, using our own hysterical energy to re-channel into destructive mayhem. Though it tried to gain our trust with tidbits about the future, even appearing to me as a school teacher (which was pretty slick considering both my mom and stepfather were teachers), its answers became increasingly ugly until it couldn't hide who it was any longer. That, however, is the point of these low-grade Demonic entities – to cause fear, then to eat the fear in the All-You-Can-Eat-Terror-Buffet. On the grand scale of dark spirits, this entity would have been considered a first-time-offender in Demon prison, still wet behind the ears. But I didn't know that yet.

Instead, I panicked because I was sure we'd let the Devil Itself into my grandparents house. And I was sure that Granny, who played organ at the Episcopal Church around the corner -- was going to kill us if we didn't get rid of this thing. I was much more afraid of Death-By-Granny than this pest.

None of the other girls seemed to know how to step in and do anything, even though I didn't really either, so we all started to say The Lord's Prayer, to send it packing the best way we knew how. I carried on with more prayers and commandments from the Bible. I figured that was the least I could do, since I made this stupid Formica Ouija Board in the first place. This had to go down in history as Worst Art Project Ever. Who knew you could make a hole to hell with a roll of scotch tape and a Sharpie?

Suddenly, POW – the green thick glass votive across the table completely exploded, as if someone had shot it with a .22 caliber bullet, right through the center. Pearl and Tracy jumped as they were pelted with the dull glass shrapnel, and bits of glass could be heard ricocheting off the paneled walls, as well as raining behind the bar. This votive had been completely obliterated, and around the candle lay glass dust. All four of us screamed and erupted from around the table, clamoring up the stairs for our lives, as fast as we could go.

To this day, the most shocking and mystical thing about the entire experience is that we didn't wake my grandparents.

As we were pounding up the stairs, I could hear with my sixth sense (or at the time, what I thought was "in my head") a laugh – a deep, gnarled belly laugh. And I could feel a presence right behind me on the stairs, something black with huge shoulders and a tiny waist. Not wearing its school teacher costume, it almost looked like a Minotaur but with a much smaller head. I could feel its breath on my back. I stayed focused on getting to the top of the stairs with the other girls and not turning around. We rounded the corner of the landing and ran into the kitchen.

It was only day two of our Formica Adventure, and our days of the Ouija Board, homemade or otherwise, were over.

We eventually got up the nerve to go back downstairs because we wanted to get to the votive glass and clean it up before poor Granny discovered the carnage and needed an explanation. We swept the glass into a bag and I tore the tiny scraps of paper off the Formica table. I used an awful lot of tape, so it took awhile, but I eventually got it all cleaned up. For years after that, I found bits and pieces of the exploding green votive in the most odd of places, all over that basement. Luckily for us – and I do mean luckily -- no evil spirit was left behind, trapped in the house. No Elemental, Inter-Dimensional, Mothman or Demon.

As we all headed upstairs after the cleaning, the quiet but brave Pearl was the last up the stairs. She turned off the basement light behind her.

"I told you guys this wasn't a very good idea."

# 4
# THE LINE IS DEAD
## WHERE: MY CHILDHOOD BEDROOM
## LOCATION: BILLINGS, MONTANA

Growing up as a Tween in Billings, my mom, stepdad and I lived in a duplex behind the fire department way out on the West End of town, right across from the gravel pit -- waiting for the right family home to come on the market. It wasn't a bad place to live by any means, yet the duplex had the personality of a box of panty liners – clean, functional, and completely nondescript. We called it home, but really, it was an affordable pit-stop until something better reared its head. We'd all made peace with this fact – as well as the sound of an occasional fire engine screaming onto 24th Street West at 1:00 am. Finally, our stay in the Panty Liner Inn was over – we received a phone call from my Grandpa's good friend Joe tipping us off that the right family home had arrived.

It was in the center of town, close to where my mom and I once lived with my grandparents shortly after my parent's divorce, right across the street from my Grandpa's best friend Joe, and around the corner from my best friend "Pearl's" house. Our new home was smack in the middle of our already-established tribe, and a welcome addition to the family. I was thrilled my parents bought the place, and I loved the big yard on the corner lot. The house was a typical 1950's architectural offering – very cute and cracker box, with two bedrooms upstairs, one bath, living room, kitchen / dining area – and a full basement with the classic thin windows that met with a view of the grass growing above. We moved in when I was in my early teens, and so of course, as an only child, I chose a bedroom in the basement, because, c'mon -- that's what teenage girls do if given the chance to create their own "nest" away from their parents.

This was quite a nest, complete with a waterbed whose frame my Grandma and Grandpa hand-stained for me. Now, you have to understand how cool a waterbed was to a teenager in the 80s. It was right up there with my tomato red $11.00 beanbag chair from Spencer's Gifts and my velvet unicorn posters. Growing up, I loved the feeling of the sloshing water. Though at the time I was unaware of the part that water plays in both purifying and amplifying an energy field, I pretended to be on a sailboat far into the Pacific Ocean – a water craft I'd most certainly purchase once I was a rich and famous actress in Hollywood. As a teen growing up in Montana, I had a lot of time to dream.

Of course, because my nest of choice was in the basement, the room came complete with paneling -- a cheap dark-walnut-print veneer glued over pressboard. Dark basement paneling was common for these homes erected in the 1950's, though this paneling was particularly hideous even by cheapie paneling standards with it's big black lines trying to pass themselves off as "paneling seams". It was definitely an interior decorating contribution made by the 1970's unhealthy obsession with dark Spanish themes (because nothing says "Romantic Spanish Galleon" like veneer). To add to the dime store design, whoever slapped up this crappy paneling didn't do a very good job, because in between the large panels were small gaps, maybe not more than a 1/16th of an inch. However, it was enough that if you looked closely, you could see the bright yellow plaster wall beneath it -- covered in haunting swirls of crayon writing. I found this unnerving. Rather than paint the walls to cover what was written, someone slapped up this dark barrier, entombing the whispers of events passed behind a quarter inch sentry of pressboard. It never did sit well with me. But, it was the 1985 – so I covered the walls and their unsettling secrets with pictures of Duran Duran and Morgan Fairchild, cranked up The Eurythmics tapes, and dressed like Molly Ringwald for school.

The truth was, that basement room – as did the whole basement – had its share of specters. The people who lived in the home prior to my family moving in had some serious problems. The home had been a rental, and the landlord decided to fix it up and put it on the market after the renters had all but trashed the place. As such, there were some oddities in the home that really stuck out – features left over once installed by the renters that the owner simply hoped would somehow go unnoticed, like a deadbolt on my basement room door that locked from the inside, only accessible with a key from the outside. That was bizarre. There were locks on the outside of the basement washroom and closet doors. The locks on the outside of both doors were placed quite high, so as to be out of a child's reach. Inside the closet, as well as low on the walls of the laundry room, was scribbled in a child's writing: "Carl was here".

It was incredibly obvious what the basement's outer locking systems were used for.

Whenever abuse of this nature takes place in any environment, that dark energy draws to it other dark entities -- just like an untreated gash on someone's arm will draw infection. There wasn't anything wrong, spiritually, with the home itself. More so, the home had been a feeding trough for Darkness for many years. Darkness was simply accustomed to dropping by, to see what was being served for dinner. Upstairs, my family's life ticked along, busy with two working parents and church on Sunday. Yet that room, interned in the ground from the rest of the home's bustling resonation, was a particular magnet for these Dark Drive-bys. Looking back, I'm sure it had something to do with the echo of atrocities that occurred there in addition to all that water (in the bed), which naturally acts as an amplifier to paranormal activity – especially if right atop underground streams, accenting a natural vortex point. It turned out that my folks dug a well right outside my basement window, and not much drilling was necessary to hit the high water table below. And, let's not forget the cherry atop this Horror Sundae – the aphrodisiac to Darkness that is the budding adolescent Psychic Medium who has no clue what her own deal is.

Yep, I experienced all sorts of paranormal activity in that room, especially Demonic attacks in dreams. It's not uncommon for young people who are just cresting into their spiritual sixth-sense abilities to end up in the crosshairs of Darkness as it makes a play for that person's spiritual alliance. After all, if Darkness can either scare or intimidate the newbie into never exploring their gifts, then that's one more bright light snuffed out in the world before it ever got started.

In one dream with a recurring theme, The Devil was calling me on the phone. I'd ignore the phone, but the ringing would get louder and louder until it was unbearable. I'd pick up in terror, knowing full well who was on the other end, only to be greeted with the most sinister and horrific screeching sound on the phone one can imagine, followed by a deep, multi-vocal-chorded laugh. Without speaking the words, both the tone and the laugh warned me very clearly: "I am coming. And you cannot stop me."

I'd wake up to a racing heart, praying into the inky darkness of my subterranean room. Good times, at sixteen.

Ten years later, I fell pale the first time I heard the Demonic screech in a place of business, the exact same screech that I'd been plagued with in my dreams. There it was, echoing throughout Kinkos in broad daylight. It had leaped from the Sandman's bag and birthed itself into reality. I'll never forget that feeling of dread that came over me as I acknowledged: It must be the time. The Devil was here. It warned me for years that It was coming, and here It was. I looked around to see if anyone else was frightened by this hideous noise, and though I saw that they, too, heard what I was hearing, it didn't have the same effect on them. I finally turned to a gentleman behind the counter and mustered the most calming tone of voice I possibly could, considering I felt like throwing up.

"Excuse me," I said, probably over correcting to the point of sounding like a demented Donna Reed, "but what's that noise?"

"Oh," he answered, as he continued stapling, "that's the modem on the computer. We're connecting to the internet."

Don't even get me started on the spiritual implications therein. That's an entirely separate book. Needless to say, it was my first lesson in prophetic imagery within dreams.

Telephones had been a recurring theme in my dreamscape since I was two years old, where a dream that repeated itself until I was seven involved a disassembled and unplugged rotary phone ringing off the hook until it was deafening – something on the other end desperate to get my attention. I later recognized this as my psyche's way of making sense of the extra-dimensional spiritual contact that I was constantly receiving. Being built like the earth's largest satellite dish is a real hayride to navigate. In any case, it was scary as heck to be a three year old watching a gutted old unplugged phone ring on a table, dream or not. So you can imagine my utter horror when, at sixteen, the real-life phantom phone calls started coming into my room at 3:00 am every morning. Of all the paranormal weirdness that happened in that basement room -- it was the phone calls that were the most upsetting.

I had one of those $7.00 phones from Spencer's Gifts (which as you can see was my Ikea back in the day) that you could hang up by simply laying it face down on a table. I was pleased with the phone's unusual lilting sing-song ringtone, a bright and piercing CHIRP-CHIRP-CHIRP-CHIRP rather than the throaty stuttering electronic pulse so prominent in early digital telephones. I also thought I was quite the technical genius by purchasing a phone jack splitter from Radio Shack – yessiree, only the best in my house – and running a phone line into my bedroom. Of course, those lame phone jack splitters did nothing but water-down the call's signal. God help the person phoning your house if more than two people picked up an extension, as there just wouldn't be enough juice in the line for anyone to hear anything. But the splitter was $1.99, which was much cheaper than $40.00 a month for an additional phone line, so I was feeling mighty proud of myself.

I've always been a night person, as that's the time when the earth rests, and I'm able to rest from the constant buzz of life. Back then, I didn't realize that I was seeking some sort of quiet on an energetic level. I just knew it was peaceful for me at night. I'd wait for quiet to fall upon the rest of the house. It was during this time that I was the most creative, writing stories and skits to bring into my drama class or drawing pictures.

I didn't envy my mom in her efforts to get me up for school the next day. I'd stay up until three or four in the morning, and then have to be resurrected at 6:30 am to get ready. I say resurrected because I slept like the dead, and by the time Friday rolled around, I'm pretty sure that I know what Lazarus felt like after Jesus gave him a hand. Considering my mom didn't have to same resources to pull from as did Jesus – again – I felt very sorry for her.

It's not as if I wanted to stay up all night. It just happened that way. And every night at 3:00 am, I would feel the ether in the room change. A tension would rise, and the air would become heavy. I would ignore this feeling, the raising of the hairs on the back of my neck and my arms, and continue doing whatever I was doing. I wasn't sure what was happening, but I always knew that it had a consciousness, and I never wanted to engage it. However, with as much denial as I wish myself into – I knew what was coming. My eyes would eventually dart over to my $7.00 Spencer's Gifts phone that was laying face-down, hung up against the phone book on the floor.

And I would wait.

What I was experiencing as an "ether change" I would later learn to recognize as not only a shift in the room's EMF (electro magnetic field) levels, but in the room's barometric pressure – thus the feeling of "heaviness". Whenever spirit life is present, it can be tracked by the EMF that it exudes – much like exhaust from the tailpipe of a car. Depending on the nature of the spirit life – whether formerly human, Elemental, or Demonic – the barometric pressure in the room will also be affected. The more inter-dimensional the entity's point of origin, the more the barometric pressure falls as the moisture in the air raises from the physics of two dimensions grinding together to create a "rip" through which the entity is able to pass. Demonic attacks are often accompanied by freak shows of water, like rain within rooms, steam across mirrors, or water trickling down the insides of windows. For Demons to manifest in our third dimension, a portal must be held open long enough for these Dark creatures to pass. Their "dimension" – or "hell", if you will – is in no way close to the resonance and vibration of our third dimension, which, for all its ills, is modeled after Light. Thus, a vacuum is created between the Light and Dark dimensions, the barometric pressure plummets, and moisture builds in the room.

This plummet was particularly apparent in my basement room, as not only would I feel my ears pop, but the moist air would cause the temperature to drop, yet I didn't recognize this at the time as a symptom of anything other than living in the basement while a Montana winter raged outside. However, even once the heating duct in the room was repaired (it never worked correctly the entire time I stayed down there) – the room still remained colder than the rest of the basement.

The digital clock clicked over to 3:01 am. My eyes quickly darted to the phone then back to my project at hand. I sat on the bed, my heartbeat starting to pick up, drawing away in a ring binder notebook to ignore the heavy feeling welling up in the room.

CH-CH-CHI... the phone stammered. It was a sickly sound, never a full ring, as if whatever was trying to come through the line didn't quite have enough signal to trip the phone's full ring response. It was a horrible sound. I continued drawing and ignored it. The air in the room was growing colder, and heavier. I drew faster.

I had, for the longest time, attempted to convince myself that every morning at 3:00 am the phone company was running some sort of test on the lines, sending some half-signal through just to make sure they were working.

But I knew that wasn't the case. Maybe tonight, it would just go away. Some nights, it wasn't as insistent as other nights. I continued to draw.

CH-CH-CH-CHI... the phone stammered again, it's Morse code of a partial ringtone breaking the silence in the room.

I looked to the phone with a good solid glance this time, and then continued my task at hand. The ethers in the room thickened to an uncomfortable point. I hunkered in – it was going to be one of those nights, a battle of wills between me and whatever kept trying to get a hold of me.

Some time had passed without the phone making a peep, and I checked the clock – 3:12 am. Maybe I had misjudged this evening's tug of war? Maybe I had –

CH-CH…CH-CH-CH… the phone chattered on the floor.

Night after night, week after week, month after month, at 3:00 am, this same thing would happen, and night after night, I'd brace for this disgusting showdown between me and something very dark that desperately wanted my attention. The closest thing I could later relate the feeling tone of this incident with was the feeling of being stalked. The worst part about it was that I had no one with whom I could share this story. Sure, I could try and tell my parents. I did in fact ask my folks if it was normal for a phone to "half ring", and my mom told me that it was probably an issue with the phone line. I let it go at that, because to get into any more depth regarding the "vibes" I was picking up, in conjunction with the wonky phone issue, waded into some murky territory. I had visions of my parents insisting that I'd lost my mind, and right after they decided to check me into the Psych wing of a Drug and Alcohol rehab unit, sure I was both drunk, high, and crazy, the phone they would have dropped off for my use – this horrible thing – would still chatter at me at 3:00 am from within my padded room in rehab.

The great irony was that in high school, I neither did drugs nor drank. I was too busy for either. I was just a budding Psychic and a Medium, and I had no idea what any of that meant except "evil, evil, evil", as stated by the Evangelical Church we were attending, which didn't have much room for anything that was out of the Pastor's interpretation of The Word. I didn't feel evil, but according to the Pastor, evil felt terrific. Well, I didn't feel terrific, either. I felt scared, and very alone in this whole pursuit. So I talked to God a lot, and hoped for the best. I figured God knew what God was doing in how I was made. Maybe one day, God would clue me in on what I was supposed to do with all that I've been given, besides stare at a $7.00 telephone in horror. That seemed a little ridiculous.

Yet there I stared.

Ch-Ch-Ch… the maniacal phone chattered in a half-ring on the floor, scratching away at the surface of my last remaining nerve like Edgar Allen Poe's swinging pendulum.

I finally couldn't take it anymore. They say people either have a fight instinct, or a flight instinct. I'm Italian, Celt, and Native American – I'll give you one guess which side of the fence I fall upon.

I reached down and grabbed the telephone up off the floor to answer. It was not the first time I'd ever done that – the first time being when I thought it may be Mountain Bell sending half-pulses out onto the phone lines to check them. I don't even know if a "phone company half pulse" is real, or if in the 1980's it was even necessary for a phone company to send electrical impulses down the lines to "check them" -- but at the time, I could tell it was some sort of energy coming through the phone line, and that lengthy explanation was the only thing that made sense to me. I pressed the phone to my ear.

"WHAT?" I barked. I had had it.

As always, the phone line was active – no dial tone, and I could hear someone was silently sitting on the other end, listening – but did not say a word. An occasional crackle or pop would come through the line.

"Hello?!" I said, braced while expecting to hear a heinous laugh that would make me regret picking up the phone.

Again, nothing but silence, and an occasional snapping that comes with the "connected" sound of "air" when someone isn't saying anything on the other end of the phone. The problem went well beyond a prank caller, who one could always hear moving, or breathing. This was a perfectly still phone call generated by something that didn't need a body. Its energy could be heard down the line with an occasional crackle or hiss. If silence had eyes, I would have felt stared down. I hung up, jumped off the bed, stormed out into the main room of the basement.

I unplugged the phone from the wall. My skin was crawling. I was done with this game.

For the first time, it occurred it me that I could unplug the phone at night, and not have to go through this. Whenever I'd pick up the phone, which wasn't very often, it was always the same – just silent air, and the very obvious resonation of someone – or something -- just listening on the other end. I actually smiled, because I couldn't believe that all this time I could have unplugged the phone, and put an end to this late night doom dance.

I whisked back into my bedroom, quickly wrapped the extra phone cable around the phone, and tossed it into a pile of teddy bears I had on my $11.00 Spencer's Gifts bean bag chair.

"There!" I said with purpose, mostly talking to break the tension in the room. "It's going to be kind of hard to call me in the middle of the night now!"

I had an enormous sense of accomplishment as I climbed back into my wavy waterbed. If there was any EMF left in the room, I wasn't able to feel it through my own adrenaline rush. I threw open my sketch pad and continued drawing.

The night wore on, and I could feel the tug of sleep pulling at me. I had moved from my drawing onto writing a dramatic monologue. I wanted to get it completed for the next day's drama class. I was in competitive drama and I often wrote my own pieces, but it was beginning to feel late. I glanced at the clock – it was 3:42 am. I started thinking about turning in to sleep when a faint, muffled sound caught my attention.

…No.

I froze. I couldn't have heard what I just heard. I just couldn't have. It was not possible.

Butterflies with spiked feet and acid covered wings exploded in my stomach. I slowly glanced over at the telephone, unplugged from the wall, wadded up in its own cord and lying wedged between grinning teddy bears. I was just too tired. I had to be too tired.

I stared silently, barely breathing, bobbing up and down as the bed rolled beneath me, the gentle lapping of the water inside the mattress filling the dead-quiet room.

…ch…ch-ch…CHIRP-CHIRP-CHIRP-CHIRP!

The telephone, wrapped in its own cord, unplugged – rang.

I don't remember how I got from the middle of a queen-sized waterbed mattress to the bottom of the staircase outside my room, but by the time I snapped to, I was barreling up the stairs with that god-forsaken telephone in my hand. I seemed to be weightless, flying to the top of the staircase in just a few hops. I was out the front door, barefoot in the snow, running for the trashcan by the driveway, the moon beating off the white blanket to illuminate my way. In one fluid movement, the trashcan lid was pulled open and I threw that phone as hard as I could into the darkness of the bin below. I heard the plastic phone explode as it hit the frozen bottom of the empty can – good -- and I wasn't going to stick around to see if a broken and unplugged telephone had the ability to ring, like it did in my dreams. I slammed the lid down and in the same weightless manner seemed to clear the sidewalk in a few steps. I was back inside, the door was locked, I ran down the stairs – dead-bolted my bedroom door behind me – and hopped into bed, pulling the covers up around my neck.

It was only when the warm water inside the mattress came into contact with the sting of my frozen feet that I realized not only was I shivering, but that I had tracked snow under my covers, as it clung to my pajama bottoms. That was okay. Everything would warm up. I wasn't getting out from beneath those covers for any reason. No matter how old a person gets, bed covers are still the only reliable monster deterrent one can truly count on.

I was in my bed, and that…thing…was outside in the trash. I pulled my Walkman from my nightstand, which was a milk crate, fumbled with my Tears for Fears "Songs from the Big Chair" cassette, and slapped the headphones on my head, turning up the volume. Under no circumstance was I going to run the risk of hearing any piercing chirpy ringtone lilting over the snow outside, echoing from the bottom of the trash can. That thing was the Golden Arm of telephones and I wasn't taking any chances. I literally said a prayer asking God to allow the possessed telephone to remain DOA, and finally, sleep took me halfway through the cassette, somewhere during the song "Listen".

The next morning came too early. My pajamas were still wet when my mom shouted down the stairs, "Danielle! Time to get up!"

After years of paranormal investigation, I came to find out that Phantom Phone Call phenomenon, though horrific, was not as uncommon as one would think. In fact, almost everything about my series of ghoulish phone calls was (paranormally) common, from the 3:00 am witching hour to the unplugged phone ringing right down to the crackling electrical presence on the other end of the call.

Phantom Phone Calls date back to the switchboard. Operators reported strange voices requesting to be patched through to their loved ones. Upon connecting the call, the Operator would be privy to the recipient's shocked reaction while hearing the voice of the dearly departed. Oddly, Alexander Graham Bell has never been lauded for his contribution to paranormal investigation. Considering how many dead people use the telephone, that's sort of a raw deal. Here's to you, Al.

But I digress.

The Phantom Phone Call phenomenon revolves around a spirit's ability to manipulate matter. A phone call is simply energy running through white noise, two things that a spirit requires in order to "speak" so that we may hear. The sheer physics of a telephone create a convenient way for spirit life to make contact from the other side. And thank God for today's unlimited data plans. (I mean, can you imagine the roaming charges on *that* call?)

In the digital era, reports have been made of people receiving mysterious cell phone calls whose ghostly number appears as either 000-000-0000 or a string of asterisks. The deceased callers are identified by their voices. Their messages tend to be brief such as "I love you" or "Goodbye". These eerie interludes rarely end with a "hang up". Instead, the chilling calls trail off into the distance or are overtaken by static until the signal disconnects. Believe me, this phenomenon is as hair-raising as it gets. Don't take my word for it -- Google "ghostly phone calls" and get ready for some chilling online EVP's and YouTube videos.

In my case, the Phantom Phone Call was not an incident involving a loved one attempting to make contact. Love had nothing to do with it. The 3:00 am hour is a traditional time for a Demonic presence to make itself known. Demons like to stick to symbols in order to mock God. It's their calling card (Demons love recognition). Demons operate around the number 3 as its a mocking of the Trinity. Demonic attacks are most common on or around 3:00 am. Sure, human entities also tend to lurk during that early morning hour when the energy of the world is still. Yet the fact that my land-line phone was able to ring *without* being plugged into the wall was indicative of something other than a human spirit. To accomplish such a feat requires an enormous amount of spiritual energy pushing through the wire. When dealing with paranormal pests, there are two entities in the spiritual realm that will pack that much fire-power: Poltergeists, and Demons.

Seeing as that Carol Ann wasn't in my room at the time, my bet was on Beelzebub.

Not to mention, my first-hand experiences with Poltergeists had not lead me to conclude that they are nothing more than the side-effects of pre-menstrual teenage girls or menopausal women. (Way to demonize the feminine, people.) Poltergeists are dark spirits, usually Demonic, that attach themselves to someone else's uncertain energy in order to utilize the chaos like a sling shot. However, they themselves are packing a good energetic punch to begin with. It's important to note that it's not the energy of the distressed person that causes the Poltergeist disturbance, but the Poltergeist itself. The Poltergeist simply fuels up on the person's discontent, "eating" the pain in order to wreak havoc. Like a bodybuilder eating protein powder before a work out, Poltergeists feast on fear. It's upsetting to me that the paranormal community persists in the belief that a hurting or distressed person is the "cause" of the Poltergeist activity. That is certainly not the case. The distressed person is a victim of an energetic bully. The "at-fault" mentality is akin to blaming the rape victim for the violent crime committed against them. As progressive as the paranormal investigative community views itself, we still have a long way to go in terms of dismissing some of the remaining spiritual folklore.

No one asks to be a Demon Buffet.

No one asks to be prank called by Hell in the middle of the night either, but that doesn't stop the calls from coming. It didn't stop the Demonic life from dropping in, either.

Unfortunately for me, this wasn't the first time Demons had decided to make a grand entrance into my childhood bedroom. Again, all budding Psychics and Mediums are a target for Darkness. If we can be frightened by the ramifications of our own abilities at a young age, we won't use them later in life for the empowerment of humanity. We'll bury our aptitudes deep within our psyche, removing ourselves from our greatest gifts. We'll become one less chess piece on the board in the match where Darkness pits itself against Light. If life were a video game, taking any one of us out of play would net a lot of points. That goes to illustrate the truly weak character of Darkness: It must pick on kids who don't yet even know who they are.

Weak or not, the most memorable grand entrance Darkness ever made into that bedroom involved my best friend "Pearl". A Demonic entity entered her body while she slept. The entity had a conversation with me and though Pearl's eyes were open -- Pearl was not home. It was so disturbing that I've actually chosen not to include the details of that particular event in this book. (Darkness doesn't need any more press than necessary). Needless to say, between help from a slew of guardian Angels and Pearl's own sense of self, we evicted the unwanted visitor from Pearl's body. When I was finally able to rouse her to consciousness, she recounted a horrible "dream" in which she wasn't herself, but something else -- something hateful -- that hated *me*. She claimed that as this "other being", she was attempting to call me on the telephone to tell me just how much she despised me. Yet in her "dream" I would never pick up.

Thank God.

I'm surprised I don't suffer from Phonophobia, after surviving countless tele-nightmares. (Yep, that's the fear of voices on the other end of a telephone and no, I didn't make it up). Telephones in a dreamscape represent our ability to receive messages from an unseen source. In the case of a budding Psychic and Medium, a telephone within a dream can also represent a "channel" we have not yet mastered.

I was a ball of un-mastered abilities back then so the recurring theme of "ringing telephones" in my dreams was all-encompassing. As a very small child between the ages of two and seven, I was plagued by a specific recurring nightmare that involved me finding my way through a post-apocalyptic wasteland. In the dream, I happened upon a shed that contained an old black rotary phone. The phone had been gutted, wires hanging everywhere, and it was lying on the table. Though the phone was disassembled and not plugged into a phone line, it would ring. In fact, it would ring so loudly that all the disassembled parts would rattle on the table. The ring was throaty and distorted and got louder with each pass- until it was so ear-splitting and terrifying -- I would wake up.

That surreal night, as I watched my unplugged $7.00 Spencer's phone chirp into a pile of grinning teddy bears, half of that wretched post-apocalyptic nightmare became manifest.

With a track record like that, I hope I never live to see the other half.

I was seventeen when the Demonic attacks ceased. I wasn't giving in, and I think the Evil Empire decided I was just not worth the trouble at that point. It was a good year or so after the Phantom Phone Call incident before I placed another telephone in my room. The replacement was a bona fide Made-In-China Spencer's Gift special, a handset in the shape of rock and roll lips. The only time the phone rang was when Pearl called. I was beyond happy about that.

I came away from that chapter of my life having learned a powerful spiritual lesson, one that I feel is crucial to pass along: Not even the Devil itself can separate a teenage girl from her telephone.

# 5
## KACHINAS IN THE MIST
### WHERE: MY AUNT AND UNCLE'S HOME
### LOCATION: TUCSON, ARIZONA

I went to college in Tucson, Arizona on a full-ride scholarship for Musical Theater. To this day my poor father insists that it was not a full-ride because when I was in college I lived with my grandparents and a "full-ride" would include the cost of housing and books. My scholarship did in fact include housing in the dorms for the entire duration of my education, but I waived the housing allotment to live with my grandparents in their amazing two story townhome in the foothills (I wasn't a stupid kid). To add to my father's confusion, budgeting was not my forte, so though I had received a chunk of money for books, I overspent and ended up calling my dad for some financial help once book buying time came along. Which is why, to this day, he is sure I'm embellishing when referring to the whole "full-ride" thing. However, the talent it takes to earn a scholarship and my ability to manage money are not on the same par. Clearly I'm much better at one than the other. So since it's a matter of public record, I encourage anyone who wishes to put an end to what has become known as "the great scholarship mystery" to contact the student union office at The University of Arizona. They can answer any of your pressing questions regarding the authenticity of my full-ride scholarship which was granted in 1987.

Yes, folks. I'm Eleventy.

The rather tragic part about the whole full-ride scholarship story was that it didn't matter anyway as I did not choose to stay in college. I left two years into the program. In fact, though I'm a huge fan of higher education for those who feel it is in line with their career paths or interests, I never wanted to attend a four-year university in the first place, much to my academic family's dismay. I wanted to get out of high school in Montana, move to LA, get a job, and immediately start auditioning for working TV or film roles. The only four year school I had any interest in attending for the purpose of reveling in the prestige of its degree was Julliard – which my family could not afford and the school offered no scholarships. The irony was that later on in life I met several people here in Los Angeles who attended Julliard, and they referred to the school as "The Jail Yard" because they claimed the curriculum was so restrictive that it discouraged the practical working efforts in the television and film industry while in school. That wouldn't have worked for me either.

I wanted to start out of high school immediately as a working actor. It wasn't as much about being famous though like any teenage girl I had big dreams of my name on a star on the Hollywood Walk of Fame. I spent large amounts of time in my math classes drawing Academy Award statues with "Danielle Egnew – Best Actress" on their #2 Lead Pencil Oscar plaques while the entire concept of Algebra flew well over my head. But really, underneath the dream of my name in glorious Hollywood lights, it was really all about making a living doing something I loved to do. All my research pointed to the fact that entertainment was best hit at a young age because it worships youth just like professional sports. This is sad but true, though for sports the issue is physicality and in entertainment the issue is aesthetics.

Talk about adding insult to injury.

Anyway, as these stories always go, my folks (who both have college degrees) did not approve of the lack of stability in the entertainment industry or the lack of stability in my plan. Naturally, they threw a fit and I just wasn't up for the fight at the ripe age of eighteen. Instead of heading to Los Angeles on my own, which was an intimidating thought for a kid from Montana with no support for a move like that, I auditioned for collegiate theater departments here and there hoping to find some sort of bridge to the next step in my life. The University of Arizona was recommended to me by my grandparents who once lived in Hardin, Montana, but now lived in Tucson after migrating south to the dry desert climate of Arizona as "full time Snow Birds" due to my grandpa's health concerns. I really loved hanging around with my grandparents. That's how I ended up at the University of Arizona. In 1987, the U of A's Musical Theater department was the fifth best in the nation, which was impressive considering it was right behind the likes of Julliard, Yale, Harvard, and USC. So my full-ride wasn't a slouchy scholarship by any means. I didn't apply for the Holy Theatrical Trinity -- Yale, Harvard, or USC -- because for as many prestigious statewide and national theatrical and musical honors I'd achieved, even I knew that my B average wasn't going to cut it with those institutions.

The problem with a degree in Musical Theater is that unless one plans on teaching, it's only good for ensuring a top management position -- at a Taco Bell or Burger King anywhere. I had no interest in the food industry, thus my choice to leave school. However, even though the U of A wasn't for me, one of the things that I absolutely loved about Tucson was the magic of the desert. And thanks to having all sorts of family that lived down there prior to my grandparent's relocation, I was able to visit my cousins as well as the desert while growing up.

The Sonoran Desert of Arizona is truly amazing – another world, full of vortexes, OffWorlders (ET's) and Ancient Elementals. Due to the electromagnetic properties in the state's ley lines, along with the high mineral concentrations underground such as copper, gold, silver, and crystalline deposits – Arizona is home to countless metaphysical phenomena. From the dimensional doorways of Sedona to the abandoned cave cities of the mysterious vanishing Anasazi tribe in Chaco canyon, Arizona is a paranormal sample-platter.

Unlike other desert habitats in America, the Sonoran Desert is unexpectedly lush with life. One usually pictures a desert to look like the barren rolling sand dunes of the Gobi in China, or the cracked ground of the desolate Mojave in California (both of which are easily mistaken for the surface of Mars). But in fact, the Sonoran Desert is unique in its geographical placement and weather patterns, receiving more rain during its flash-flood monsoon season than other deserts. The result is a fantasy world of stinging space-alien plant life and really weird looking animals, like giant, misshapen furry spiders that resemble the creative inspiration for those terrifying larvae that pop out of the eggs and latch onto people's faces in the *Alien* movies. Or, let's not forget the Javalina: a bristly pig-thing in the boar family whose humongous head and disturbingly long werewolf teeth are eclipsed only by curly tusks that look like they have more in common with the extinct North American Mammoth than – well – a pig.

The seductive mystery of the Sonoran Desert touches many of our lives every day and we're barely aware of it. For instance, I'm sure you've heard of mesquite, the flavorful woodchip that adds a specific level of glee to any barbequed rib product. Did you know that the Mesquite Tree is indigenous to the Sonoran Desert and its unique climate? Well it is. And did you know that though it looks like any other mid-sized tree upon first glance, what appears to be "a leaf" is actually dozens of teensy-tiny leaves, as to not let precious water evaporate out of the tree and into the arid desert? A Mesquite Tree looks like something that fell out of *Jurassic Park*, right next to another Sonoran Desert botanical icon you'll likely recognize from countless Westerns: the Saguaro Cactus, or better known by most laymen as "that tall cactus with arms". Saguaro can only be found in this unique climate anomaly. Due to the lack of rain between the monsoons, it takes these Saguaro Cacti, which can reach a height of 50 feet, close to 100 years to sprout their signature arms. A Saguaro Cactus can live for up to 200 years. Because of the antiquity of these cacti it is illegal in Arizona to cut down a Saguaro Cactus. The Arizona city planners will actually plot commercial roadways *around* patches of Saguaro, resulting in quite a few winding roads in Tucson such as Campbell Avenue that snake down the foothills of the Catalina Mountains like one of the tracks in Disneyland's Matterhorn ride.

The State of Arizona actually employs people to relocate Saguaro Cacti. I'm not sure who takes these jobs, considering the obvious downside, but these people exist. Fearless folks attempt to avoid the two-story tower of three inch spines to gingerly harness these multi-ton monsters. Saguaro Cacti are not only incredibly tall but insanely heavy, full of water-storing pulp with a circumference of up to ten feet. Extreme care must be taken in craning the Saguaro onto a flatbed truck. One slip while being loaded and the cactus will be splattered into mush on the roadway under its own weight – hundreds of years of life gone in an instant.

Great planning is taken in the relocation of a Saguaro Cactus, as Horticulturists must ensure that the new terrain nearly matches the old terrain and won't void the established 200 year-old-root system of nutrients by planting it next to other species that will fight for the desert's precious supply. The care and reverence given to a Saguaro Cactus by the State of Arizona is almost religious, and it makes sense – these cacti are one of the oldest living entities on earth. And when you're in the presence of a Saguaro, towering above you with its three or four arms saluting the sunset – you are definitely in the presence of a conscious being. We simply may not understand the consciousness.

But that's not the fault of the cactus -- 200 years our senior.

One of my very favorite Saguaro Cacti lived on a plot of land owned by my Aunt and Uncle in Tucson. This cactus was a comparative newbie and was just starting to sprout two different arms, which were making their appearance as nubs on either side of the spine-covered-rocket. Just like people, all Saguaro have very distinct personalities. If you quiet yourself to listen, you can hear their whispers.

I first became acquainted with this cactus upon arriving at my Aunt and Uncle's' when I was in my teens. It lived in what would be considered their front yard, only in Tucson, especially in the foothills, "yards" meant "whatever was naturally there in the desert to begin with". Unlike Phoenix (or what I like to call "Los Angeles East"), which is obsessed with attempting to plant lawns in spite of the crippling lack of water, Tucson utilizes the glory of the natural plant life in the Sonoran Desert in planning the landscaping for housing developments. Home sites are chosen in a subdivision based upon the least amount of foliage that needs to be cleared and away they go. It's a rather ingenious method of working with the land and the climate.

My buddy the Saguaro sat right outside my Aunt and Uncle's front door and would often be wrapped in Christmas lights around the holidays. That was kind of cool. It was adorable how much the cactus loved being strung with those decorations. That Saguaro was extremely eager and would always toss me a "Hi! Hi! HI!" every time I arrived. Now, I assumed that everyone was communing with the cactus just as I was. I mean, how could anyone miss this thing? It had more personality than a teacup Chihuahua.

I came to find out that most people, though they could feel something was extraordinary about these succulents, could not hear them. That rare but slightly embarrassing ability fell somewhere within my pile of sixth senses and I surely was not going to go around touting my identity as The Cacti Whisperer (I had enough problems blending in as it was). Besides, it wasn't as if I heard an audible voice. It was more like the Saguaro beamed me the energy of what it was saying, along with a corresponding emotional response that I could relate with a facial expression.

In other words -- Saguaro Cacti are extremely telepathic.

Before you poo-poo the idea of a telepathic plant – and I suppose I wouldn't blame you if you did -- let me draw your attention to the jellyfish. Jellyfish have no brain and no eyes -- at least, according our human understanding of what makes up a brain and what makes up eyes. In fact, we aren't even able to locate a nervous system for these creatures, or any nerves at all. No veins, no heart, and no internal organs besides a crude stomach, which doesn't even work like a stomach. We aren't even exactly sure how the jellyfish is able to sense prey in the water. Yet, these creatures will communicate with each other and intelligently choreograph a group hunting endeavor, making split-second and cunning decisions as a pack. They are acutely aware of their surroundings, and attempt to flee as predators are in their midst long before they are attacked. Yet to us, they look like nothing more than aimless tapioca desserts, undulating in the sea.

Good Lord. I wonder what we look like to them?

Jellyfish, like Saguaro Cacti, are primarily made of water. And, like the Saguaro, they are also telepathic communicators. We humans are also primarily water, and I think that has a great deal to do with our ability to telepathically communicate with these entities as water is sensitive to vibration. My favorite display at The Aquarium of the Pacific in Long Beach, CA, is the Jelly Room, where amongst other species one can find a Moon Jelly tank that is breathtaking. Floor to ceiling, this round, clear tank is roughly eight feet in diameter. The jellies float in the midst. I was drawn to this tank because of the resonation that comes off of these jellies in particular. It almost felt like music -- gentle wind chimes rocked by the breeze but without the sound to carry the notes. I stood in front of the Moon Jelly tank for quite some time, mesmerized by this musical pulse and their movement until I locked into it. I realized that they were acknowledging me as they swam by, because they could hear me too. Some of them would do special flexing movements to say hello. I wasn't touching the thick Plexiglas, but I was standing close enough that I felt as though I could float in the tank with them. Almost ten minutes had passed with me just vibing with the jellyfish, and I was unaware that a large number of jellies were clumped together in front of me -- just hovering there. I was jarred out of my hypnotic stasis by a woman who commented, "Wow, they sure like you." As soon as I was made conscious of the fact that I was standing on the outside of the tank, I could feel that hypnotic telepathic connection start to slip away. The jellies slowly began undulating back into the tank, their movement accompanied by little musical voices that said, "Bye-bye! Bye-bye!"

For something whose sting is so painful, they are delightful creatures.

The most impacting aspect of the Moon Jelly experience was the overall feeling with which I was left -- one of such relaxation, oneness, and peace. Saguaro Cacti have a similar feel, though theirs is rooted in a low-pulse antiquity that is more in line with the pulse of the earth. The older the cactus, the more austere and more powerful is its presence.

The Saguaro with nine and ten arms, 200 years old, is often disinterested in even communing with us. Their consciousness has become one with something so much bigger than we are that their ability to comprehend is much larger than ours. Extremely old Saguaro almost feel "cold" because of this disconnection. The fact is – we're just too pea-brained to be on their radar at this point in their centuries of evolution. There are so many of God's creations that we don't understand – far more than we do actually – that we'd be better off as a species to just toss our hands in the air and say:

"I dunno."

The desert is full of creatures with which we don't really have anything in common and so I was relatively glad to have my Aunt and Uncle's perky front-yard Saguaro as my buddy. One summer when I was around fifteen years old, I was staying with my cousin "Tracy" out in the family's guest house. It was a mother-in-law's house that was right off the pool and we felt like complete rock stars out there with our own space, our refrigerator stocked with huge five-gallon containers of Baskin Robbins ice cream – pralines and cream. I remember losing ten pounds that summer, an ironic accomplishment while living on Basking Robbins and bbq'ed chicken breasts. I suspect the fact that we never got out of the pool had something to do with the mystery weight loss.

It was teenage girl heaven.

Tracy and my Aunt had to go into town for something, and my Uncle was working on a project out of the house. So, I volunteered to stay behind at the homestead while the family went out to do what they needed to do. I had a silver Montgomery Ward boom box that I was particularly proud of because it had a dual tape deck. Back in the day, that meant the freedom to duplicate tapes. The possibilities to one's music collection were endless if you had the time. As a teenager in the 80's, one did not take into consideration the money that we were taking out of an artist's or record label's pocket by copying a tape. That awareness came later with Napster. In fact, back in the day, the record labels weren't as touchy about tape-to-tape consumer pirating, though they weren't thrilled about it – mostly because it was not only time consuming to copy each tape in real time while listening, but the quality of the duped tape was crummy. Unlike mp3's, which can be ripped in an instant, sound as pristine as the CD, and can be passed around a million times with the click of a mouse, the duped tape took nearly an hour to complete, had to be hand-labeled and physically handed to a pal, and was inevitably "hissy" compared to the original -- which hissed in the first place, thanks to the nature of analog sound. Yet back then, we didn't know the difference so, as teenagers, we really thought we were livin' large with the duped tape thing.

I picked the den for my tape-duping endeavor. It was a small and quiet room on the end of the home full of big windows. The room had an interesting high vibration that I found to be very peaceful. It turns out that there was a reason the resonation in the room was so high: My Aunt and Uncle were the only people I knew who practiced New Age spirituality, and they meditated in the den. Viola – high vibration. I never saw them meditate nor was I interested in the thought of sitting in one place for a long time with my eyes closed. But, like praying, I understood that remaining quiet was important in spiritual matters – so I let the whole idea of mediation fall into the category of "things adults do" – and continued to listen to The Police.

The den, though peaceful, had one downside: I always had the feeling that an unseen set of eyes was watching me. This feeling was always present, even if Tracy and I were hanging out in the den together. Of course, when Tracy was there I dismissed this feeling, because where two or more teenage girls are gathered, nothing can tear them asunder. However, in the room all by its lonesome, this feeling was a touch unnerving. It was a sensation of "trespassing", or rather that something felt that I was trespassing. Now, let it be known that this feeling of "trespassing" is not unique in the Sonoran Desert, so I wasn't in a panic about it. It was a very familiar though slightly uncomfortable sensation that would come over me while hiking through various areas. I attributed it to Saguaro who just weren't in the mood to chat or who would send out a prohibitive pulse to warn me about scorpions or other poisonous creatures waiting for me on the path beyond – danger, Will Robinson. (Saguaro Cacti are extremely helpful for the most part). If I knew then what I know now, I would have also taken into account the enormous amount of nature spirits present in the desert that will often attempt to dissuade a careless hiker from pursuing their path. Elementals, God's "middle management" accountable to Mother Nature, are very committed to protecting their environment. But I wasn't terribly aware of such creatures – only the energetic warning shots they'd fire across my bow, urging me to stop climbing on fragile rocks, or walking across a wash area where delicate plant life struggled to sprout. Growing up in the wilds of Montana, I was very conservation oriented. Yet even I needed an education on the nuances of desert flora and fauna, and even more, an education on staying out of the crosshairs of the desert's unique energized ley lines.

To distract myself from this all-too-familiar trespass resonation that was building in the den, I got up off the floor (where I'd set up the tape duping factory) and decided to look over the contents of the shelves. It was a miniature museum and I welcomed the distraction. My Aunt and Uncle had some really fantastic Native American art in their home and this room particularly held some terrific pieces – authentic Hopi pottery, the kind you only touch with your eyes because it cost a small fortune, and tiny but ornate Navajo baskets of woven pine needles. There were plates of colored sand, reproducing the pink panoramic deserts sunsets, and on one shelf stood the figurines.

They were my favorite.

I asked my Aunt about the figures the first time I saw them. Standing not quite a foot high, they were the most quizzical things I'd seen in a long time. Fabricated from what looked like painted clay, wood, and authentic animal hides, these figures were akin to a brown Ken doll from the shoulders down, wearing either tiny leather loin cloths or draped skins made of rabbit fur. Where they had no clothing, their bodies were painted with tribal swirls or bold plots of color. In their clenched hands were staffs topped with spear heads or some with delicate feathers. Some held drums, and some held shields. The workmanship on these dolls was amazing, and they were not encouraged to be touched. (I later found out that the dolls can go for several thousand dollars). Yet it was their head that really was the what-the-heck focal point. The head looked as if a cave painting had been cross with a buffalo, or a bird of prey, or sometimes, a really stylized totem pole face. Half impressionistic and half animalistic, these creatures didn't look like men wearing masks, but something else – something mystical. They weren't frightening but they weren't exactly inviting. I was fascinated by the fact that no matter which doll I was focused on – none of them were really that friendly looking, but each one was interesting in its own way.

When I asked my aunt about the creepy-cool dolls on the shelf, she told me that they were representations of kachinas. I was informed that kachinas are a prevalent part of Southwestern Pueblo Native American Spirituality. When I asked her what they were, as in, what they stood for, she had a harder time answering me. She came out with "a spirit", and when I asked if they were like an angel, she smiled and shook her head, answering "Not exactly."

In her defense, describing the concept of a kachina to a Westernized Christian is tough because, unlike the defined spiritual concept of only one God and a set of Angels, just about anything in creation can be represented as a kachina. I mean anything at all in the physical world, or even the spiritual one, from a spirit protector to a deceased loved one. But a kachina doesn't have to be an entity, or even a live object. It could represent a mood ("sorrow"), a quality in a human being ("virtue"), a naturally occurring phenomenon like the stars, the sun, the moon, rice, birds, animals, insects, or a thunderstorm. Kachinas are, in effect, a physical representation of anything's mojo, personified. In the personification process, Kachinas have relationships like any humans would -- they themselves have family members, like aunts and uncles, and even sometimes children. Kachinas were the modality used by ancient peoples to make sense of, and feel connected to, the energies of all living things around them.

There are over 400 kachina representations in the Hopi Pueblo alone. So how in the heck my poor Aunt was supposed to explain this full-service spiritual concept to a hopelessly Judeo-Christian niece who at the time was attending an Evangelical church I'm not sure. Yet she gave it a college try, and explained that though kachinas are not worshipped, each is viewed as its own powerful force who, if given respect and petitioned, would use their respective mojo to bless the person with their specific strength. (Sort of like how Catholic folks petition St. Christopher, the Patron Saint of lost items, to help find the car keys). For instance, a kachina that represents the spirit of corn, if petitioned, would bring success to crops. A kachina that represents the spirit of rain, if petitioned, would bring a storm. Basically, kachinas personify the life force and connectedness in all things, and the need for human beings to commune and connect directly with this life force so as not to perish in perceived separation from our surrounding Universe.

Again, I'm not sure how much of this information my aunt thought would stick with me, as my spiritual background consisted of 1) The Father, 2) The Son, and 3) The Holy Ghost. Technically, kachinas would sort of fall into category three – very, very loosely. Kachinas are more akin to spiritual representations found in other indigenous world religions like the Fey – or Faeries – of Ireland. The indigenous Celtic religions believed that everything in nature had a life force, and that life force was sacred. Modern Wicca is based upon this principle. It makes sense that an ancient people in the Southwest would create small figurines to help remember that all energy can be solicited for help. In Western religious practices, the closest counterpart to the kachina are the Catholic Saints who are petitioned for assistance.

All of this information fully explained why the kachina dolls were so strange-looking – a Ken doll meets the Island of Dr. Moreau after having an affair with a hieroglyph. I loved the idea of a spiritual entity that couldn't quite be described but could bless you with something cool depending on your need. I asked if they were all tiny, like the dolls – hey, I didn't know – and my aunt informed me that since a kachina could represent anything, its size could vary, too.

That afternoon in the room, all by myself, I studied these kachina dolls intently, thinking about what the kachina of music would look like as The Police played in the background. As I pondered Sting in a loin cloth with a cave painting for a head, the feeling of being watched became unbearable. Something was standing in the periphery of the room, looking at me from the doorway. It was too uncomfortable to ignore. I couldn't stand it anymore so I shot a glance to the open door. I could feel the presence looking at me back, but I couldn't see it. We stayed in what felt like a stare down, and I felt presence finally step away from the doorjamb and disappear. I was relieved and dismissed this incident as my own imagination going wild after staring at wonky looking dolls. Deep down I knew that wasn't the case, but I was alone in the house and, even though it was broad daylight, the denial made me feel better.

I left the land of the kachina – known as my aunt's upper shelf – and went back to labeling my tapes. Tracy was going to flip when she saw the bounty of music I was providing her. Just moments later, I felt something peering down through the ground level window behind me – from the outside. I snapped my head around, as anyone would when they feel someone staring at them through a window, only to find nothing there. The presence had once again moved.

I thought to myself, "Great, there's some kind of ghost walking around the outside of the house. Next it will look at me through –"

Just as I started to think "through the other window", a shadow cast over the floor coming from the last widow to my left. I leaped to my feet as the shadow fell across me and my pile of tapes, and I looked to the window – surely it must be the gardener or the pool man -- but there was no one there.

At this point, I was completely freaked out. How can something cast a shadow, but be invisible? It was a beautiful Arizona afternoon outside -- the sun was streaming onto the window seat and onto the floor, and here was this person-esque shaped shadow on the floor at my feet, but no person. How was that possible? I made sure to step out of where the shadow fell – that was just too weird, as who the heck knew what that shadow could do? What if it was some Peter Pan shadow with an independent personality? Finally the shadow moved off, just as if someone who had been standing at the window continued to walk on.

At this point, I was really regretting my decision to stay at home by myself.

I froze. The air was charged. I wanted to bolt out of the room but I was afraid to leave. What if I ran into whatever it was around the corner? I could feel my own adrenaline pumping, and my eyes fell back to the doorway because I was sure that if whatever this was had made a round past the windows, its next stop would be back to the door. All was quiet, but I wasn't going to turn my back to either window or that doorway. Though I wasn't really accepting of my Psychic abilities yet as I hadn't ever actually heard of such a thing, I began doing what I always did – decoding the energy of whatever this thing was. In truth, I had no idea what it was. Usually, spirits have a former gender to which they adhere in their awareness of themselves. This was neither male nor female. It was neither happy nor sad. It was neither menacing nor inviting.

If anything, it was curious.

Suddenly, the most deafening sound burst through the ceiling from the roof – BOOM BOOM BOOM BOOM – four HUGE footsteps from one corner of the room to the other cut right above my head. Whatever was walking across the roof had to be enormous to clear that room, corner to corner, in just four strides. And it had to be incredibly heavy, as each step sounded as if a boulder was being dropped. I could hear the roof beams crack under the weight of each colossal step, and pictures jiggled on the wall.

It wasn't an earthquake. Earthquakes don't travel across the rooftop from one corner of the room to the other. Earthquakes don't cause the timber in the ceiling to crack and pop under each individual BOOM as whatever it was stepped across the roof.

I shot out of that room like I'd been nailed in the tailbone with a cattle prod.

Out into the living room, my heart was racing and I was staring at the doorway to the den. The boom box was still playing from inside, oblivious to the fact that an invisible giant just ran across the roof. There was something extra eerie about the music continuing on none the wiser. I had absolutely no intention of going in there to shut it off.

Once I was out of the den, the uncomfortable feeling of being watched was gone. Now calming down, I was instantly aware of what that whole display was all about. Whatever had been staring at me from the doorway and though the windows had wanted me out of that den. It wasn't an angry or vengeful feeling, but more a protective feeling. After it tried staring me down to get me to leave and even casting a shadow on me, it had no other choice but to resort to something a little more dramatic. I'm extremely sensitive to tones, and loud noises will about put me through the roof. (No pun intended, but I wish it would have been – that was pretty good). Whatever this entity was knew this fact about me and loud sounds. So, after trying everything to get me to leave, it had to resort to some heavy lifting. Or in this case, some really, really, really heavy stepping.

After I realized the whole display was to get me to exit the den, images flooded into my mind's eye as this gatekeeper made itself known to me. I smiled. It was a kachina belonging to the den. No wonder I had been drawn to the shelves in the den containing the strange-looking dolls – this kachina had been attempting to make itself known to me in any way it could. I could now "see" the kachina, kneeling on one knee atop the roof. It was enormous, twelve or fourteen feet tall, the massive head and shoulders looking like an ancient bison with the beak of a bird of prey, and round black stones for eyes. It was draped in layers of heavy pelts, its skin a powdered grey color. Its feet were wrapped in boots of fur up to its knees. In one hand it held what looked like a rattle or shaker made of some sort of painted gourd. It stared at me through the roof with its obsidian eyes, letting me know that its job was to keep the meditation space pure. I was a stranger inside the den, pirating tapes. There's nothing pure about that. The kachina was likely asked to act as a protector by my Aunt and Uncle who would wish removal of any wrong vibration from the sanctuary.

I hung my head, a little embarrassed. The music was still blaring from the den. I laughed out loud to break my own tension, and edged back toward the doorway. "Okay, listen," I said, my hands held high as if this kachina was afraid I'd pull a gun from my sweater pocket, "I'm going to go in and get my stuff and bring it to the living room. Please don't run across the roof again. That was really loud."

I waited a moment, reaching deep into my psyche to pull up a fistful of courage, and walked quickly into the room. I could feel this gigantic entity kneeling on the roof, staring straight down at me through the timbers as I scurried to get my items. Every second I was there I feared the hideous BOOM that had just sent me packing. I quickly yanked the boom box cord from the wall by its cable, scooped the clacking pile of tapes up with one hand and snagged the boom box with the other and walked briskly out of the den and into the corner of the living room.

In the quiet of the house, I could feel this kachina recede back into the ethers and into the desert floor. The startling interaction with me wasn't personal. I just wasn't supposed to be doing what I was doing in the space I was doing it in.

I stopped duping tapes for the day.

When my cousin Tracy came home, I told her about the incident but without getting into detail about the kachina part. I felt that might've been a little "out there". She told me that she didn't care for that area of the house either because she felt watched too – but from inside the den. The den emptied into a small washroom where the washer and drier were housed, and that room emptied into the living room. I'd sprinted through the small washroom to get to the living room. I didn't know at the time that large EMF (Electro Magnetic Field) bursts will cause people to feel watched, and one of the leading causes of large EMF emissions is a poorly grounded 210 volt wall socket used for the drier. Many "hauntings" are said to take place in washrooms, most of which are just our brain responding to the EMF leak from badly grounded wiring. All that being said, this incident was definitely not a mental trick caused by electrical interference. EMF doesn't run across a roof or jiggle pictures on the wall from the impact.

I gave Tracy the tapes I'd finished and she was thrilled. We didn't hang out in the den any further that trip.

I had other paranormally interesting things happen in that house, like prophetic dreams and hearing a male giggle in the hallway as I was getting ready in the bathroom one morning. The latter was a little unnerving, as I heard footsteps approach the open bathroom and stop, just inches around the corner, as if someone were holding their breath, hoping I wouldn't notice them. Again, I was in the house by myself. I quickly poked my head out into the hallway and saw nothing, though I could feel someone inches from my face. In my mind's eye I then saw that he was wearing a dark blue military uniform from the 1800's. He seemed okay, as ghosts went. At least he was happy. As it turned out, he thought I was cute and, with the giggle, was doing his best to flirt from the other side. How can a gal be offended by that kind of effort?

Before I left to return home to Montana, I asked my buddy the Saguaro Cactus if the house was haunted. The cactus didn't know what haunted meant. I tried to explain that it meant "dead people walking around". The cactus didn't understand the difference between a flesh-and-blood person with a soul and a soul. To the Saguaro, as long as the soul was illuminated, it was alive. I had to rephrase my question to ask the cactus if there were many people in the home who had a soul, but didn't have a flesh and blood container for the soul. The cactus told me that yes, there were many. The home had been on an old sheep trail that had been adopted for use by the military, and many people had expired along the long and hot trek. I came to find out from my Uncle that the winding roadway that emptied into El Camino Road – the street the house was built upon -- had indeed, been a sheep trail.

That cactus knew its stuff.

So, in reference to my full-ride scholarship -- I did receive quite an education while in Arizona. It's just that little of my education took place at the University.

# 6
## LITTLE PEOPLE IN THE BIG SKY
### WHERE: THE RIMROCKS
### LOCATION: BILLINGS, MONTANA

They don't call Montana the Big Sky Country for nothing. When there's a lot of sky, there's a lot than can happen within it. All one has to do is look up. That is, if a person dares. In a place like Montana, where spinning a yarn is only admirable if one owns sheep, it's always best to tell the truth. Even if the truth is a bitter pill to swallow.

Stories of contact with what I've termed as OffWorlders (because I think "alien" is just rude) have weaved through human history. We see evidence of humanity's fascination with life beyond the stars documented as far back as the Mayan culture. The stone sarcophagus lid belonging to the Mayan Palenque ruler, Pacal the Great, was meticulously carved to portray him flying off into the afterlife – in a capsule-like rocket that he himself is operating, complete with fire spurting out the back, levers and pedals to operate, and a hose connected to his nose. Nice that he could rig up some oxygen – I hear the vacuum of space wreaks havoc on the bronchial system.

Then there are the hieroglyphs in the 3,000-year-old temple of Pharaoh Seti I in Abydos, Egypt that depict what look exactly like aircraft -- a perfect representation of a helicopter, a classic airplane, and even what looks clearly like a modern yacht or tanker. These unmistakable glyphs are not referenced anywhere else in any Egyptian language. The glyphs completely baffled Victorian-era archeologists in 1848 -- none of whom had ever seen an airplane or a helicopter. Egyptologists attempted to debunk these etchings as "typos", as it was common back in the day for one Pharaoh to take over and carve over the top of someone else's writings, resulting sometimes in confusing garble underneath. It wasn't until identical glyphs depicting the same helicopter and other planes were found in the 3,000 year old temple of Amon Ra in Karnak – approximately 55 miles (89 km) away -- that the glyphs were not interpreted as "typos".

Can someone say "Bermuda Triangle"?

The Hindu religion even weighs in on the concept of OffWorlders making contact with humanity with its own mythology documented in the Ramayana, a religious text that dates back to the 5th century BC. The gods of the time were said to have transported themselves in flying chariots, or "flying cars" called Vimanas, to bring knowledge down to humanity from the heavens. And of course, let's not forget the Mesopotamian carving of the Cylinder Seal, depicting ancient Sumarians communing with a cigar-shaped craft hovering with wings beneath it, while little bitty creatures sit atop the craft.

Because that's not creepy.

There are the world-famous Nazca Lines of Peru, which are gigantic figures etched in the dirt of the high desert plateaus and can only be viewed in their entirety from high up in an aircraft. Including a giant monkey and a huge spider, one of the most noted of these figures is the representation of a humanoid creature with a big head, huge eyes, and a small body -- what we would consider a shoe-in for the modern-day Grey Alien. The monkey and the spider are pretty spot-on in their literal artistic depiction, so it's very doubtful that the image of this little alien critter is some sort of sudden impressionist interpretation of an ancient Peruvian. Unless, of course, ancient Peruvians looked like characters from the *Peanuts* cartoon, and perhaps all this time, Charles Shultz has been channeling this long-lost human physiology in his pen-and-ink portrayal of Peppermint Patty. But my money's on ET's for this one, as there were no hydrocephalic monkeys carved into the hillsides.

And let's not forget to the most obvious citation of "something" being seen in the night sky: The Biblical account of Ezekiel and his wheel, written between 583 and 565 BC:

### Ezekiel 1:4-6 (NIV)

*4 I looked, and I saw a windstorm coming out of the north—an immense cloud with flashing lightning and surrounded by brilliant light. The center of the fire looked like glowing metal, 5 and in the fire was what looked like four living creatures. In appearance their form was human, 6 but each of them had four faces and four wings.*

### Ezekiel 1:15-21 (NIV)

*15 As I looked at the living creatures, I saw a wheel on the ground beside each creature with its four faces. 16 This was the appearance and structure of the wheels: They sparkled like topaz, and all four looked alike. Each appeared to be made like a wheel intersecting a wheel. 17 As they moved, they would go in any one of the four directions the creatures faced; the wheels did not change direction as the creatures went. 18 Their rims were high and awesome, and all four rims were full of eyes all around.*

*19 When the living creatures moved, the wheels beside them moved; and when the living creatures rose from the ground, the wheels also rose. 20 Wherever the spirit would go, they would go, and the wheels would rise along with them, because the spirit of the living creatures was in the wheels. 21 When the creatures moved, they also moved; when the creatures stood still, they also stood still; and when the creatures rose from the ground, the wheels rose along with them, because the spirit of the living creatures was in the wheels.*

Though one may remain skeptical about whether or not life on other planets exists, one cannot deny odd and recurring themes of "flying cars" and "space people" that crops up throughout human history, long before George Jetson and his boy Elroy hit the Saturday Morning Cartoon circuit.

I always had an acute awareness that something, or rather more accurately – someone -- was "out there". I've been a sky-watcher from day one, spending precious quality time plunked in a hammock late at night in my grandparents' back yard back in Billings, Montana, my eyes glued to the heavens. In Montana, there was no light pollution, with such a sparse population, and stars in the heavens were more difficult to single out, as the sky looked more like someone had spilled an overflowing cup of salt all over a piece of black construction paper. The outer arms of The Milky Way were clearly visible, the million-mile wide gaseous clouds looking like a huge bluish-white feather boa plume draped across the center of the summer sky. In Montana, the sky was so large (Big Sky Country, don't you know), that you could actually see the curve of the Milky Way itself as it wrapped it's way across the galaxy. It was, and still is – breathtaking.

My Grandpa would sit in one aluminum lawn chair and my Grandma in the other, the red-orange cherries of their cigarettes glowing in the darkness under the apple tree while my Grandpa explained to me how to spot satellites in the thick field of stars. I loved spending time with my grandparents like this. Not much was said on these occasions in the quiet of the night, beneath the grandeur of a universe so large that one would practically pop an aneurism trying to take it all in. But at the same time, it was in this silence that everything was said.

I'm a firm believer that my Grandpa believed in ET's and UFO's as well, but we never really talked about the reality of any of it, outside of my Grandpa's usual over-the-top sense of humor about Martians coming to eat everyone's brains, which was often followed by my Grandma's sharp reprimand about not scaring the grandkids. But we were never scared. We all knew what hip my Grandpa was shooting from. My Grandpa was a sharp and creative man, and like many of his generation who came from financially modest families – Grandpa's parents immigrated to America from Italy and settled as farmers in Billings -- he channeled his big brain not into higher education, but into brilliant blue collar entrepreneurialism. In my Grandpa's case, it was carpentry. He was able to design and build anything out of wood – including toys for all of us grandkids. My mom and I lived with my grandparents, so I really received the lion share of these late-afternoon projects in Grandpa's garage. Upon special request from me, he constructed an amazing flying saucer built upon an old rotisserie that he braced vertically, so when the steel rotisserie arm was run through the middle of the UFO, and the rotisserie engine was plugged in, the wooden UFO appeared to rotate and hover, the eerie hum of the rotisserie engine adding ambiance. To top off this masterwork, Grandpa glued panels of colored cellophane all around the periphery of the UFO, and fastened a trap door in the bottom, through which a flashing light was placed up into the belly of the craft. The result was a slow rotating, multi-colored flashing UFO that by adding a few Star Wars figures or Micronauts up into the belly of the hull through the trap door, to cast creepy silhouettes against the cellophane for effect, made the most outstanding toy in the world to play with in the dark.

Montana is known as Big Sky Country because the sky looks incredibly huge. This may not make any sense, because technically speaking, the sky is the same size no matter where anyone is located, geographically -- but if you ever travel there and look up, you'll instantly understand. It really is uncanny. Montanans grow up as Children of the Sky, and we spend a great deal of time looking up into this enormous expanse above. I've known many Montanans who have reported seeing unusual lights moving about in the atmosphere, and have even recounted first-hand experience standing face to face with brilliantly lit craft hovering feet above farmland. Keep in mind that the brass-tacks culture of Montana doesn't really support people spinning paranormal stories – especially about little green men. So when these UFO stories would come from grizzly old-school farmers whose life-aged faces had been forged into that of an Apple Head Doll, those stories command one's full attention.

In 2010, one of my good friends from back home, a non-metaphysical *Lonesome-Dove*-type-of-guy, told a story of lying in his bed only to be awakened by a very bright light hovering above a radio tower by his rural-area home. He described the light as oval-shaped, more oblong, glowing bright white as it hovered three feet above the ground. He felt as though it was attempting to get his attention. My friend is a religious person, so when I brought up the idea of UFO's, he said that he choose to believe it was some other prompt from God, the implication being perhaps angels. However, angelic re-frame or not, I could tell that my friend didn't know what to make out of it, and he didn't really want to revisit the topic.

What I found even more interesting was that this same friend had shared with me that his father, who is the typical no-nonsense old-timer one would expect to find in the dustbowls of Eastern Montana, had told of an experience where he came face to face with a very large craft in a field. The old-timer said that this craft hovered just above his head for about 15 minutes, brilliant with different colored lights, and that the craft was very aware that he was below, just staring straight at it. Considering this old-timer is as non-spiritual as they come, and considering he risked being laughed out of every bar from his tiny hometown to the North Dakota border for telling such an outlandish story – I took the account seriously. I explained to my friend that it was not uncommon for UFO's to either abduct, or track through communication of some kind, a family line – much like how modern scientists today will tag sea turtles and monitor their movement.

My friend didn't really have a comment about that.

Overall, Montanans don't have comments on UFO activity, even when they are experienced by themselves. When I was around 20 years old, I came back to Montana from a few years of college in Arizona. I was making a pit stop back home, trying to figure out what I wanted to do next with my life. I had decided that college was not for me, and I'd left the University of Arizona. Upon arriving back to Montana, I was greeted with a non-stop barrage of appeals from my parents to give college one more shot. It was relentless. And considering I was living with my mother, who was not only a teacher at the time but is also

Italian -- the level of "suggestion" was at an all-time high. These "suggestions" ranged from "trying a smaller school" (the University of Arizona had 45,000 students) to the fact that my Uncle, with whom I really got along, had started back to college to finish his degree in search of a second career later in life, so I could attend with him. Well, needless to say, when even my childhood friend "Jake" was attending Eastern Montana College – which has since been turned into Montana State University-Billings – I caved under the peer pressure.

Not having a better plan at the moment, I figured I could hang with my Uncle and Jake at the student union building. I tried out for, and received, another scholarship in Theater. I really gave Eastern a college try – pun completely intended this time. I earned an "A" in Puritan Literature -- a class that my twisted friend Jake had bribed me into registering for with promises of bringing me hot coffee and a ride to class every morning. He valiantly lived up to his end of the agreement. The Puritan Lit class was a thrill a minute, soaking in "Sinners in the Hands of an Angry God" at 7 a.m. My hard-earned "A" plummeted once the professor sprang an impossible final on the entire class, who all failed across the board. The book for this class was 2,000 pages of bible-thin paper, all containing the most painfully dry and hideously boring American literature to ever have the misfortune of being preserved. Each Puritan writer had the same "voice" as the next, as, well – they were Puritans. "Standing out" wasn't really encouraged. The final exam, which was going to count for half our grade, consisted of five pages of obscure one-sentence quotes. We were to cite the author of the quote, and the work from which it came – drawing upon 2,000 bible-thin pages of near-identical material -- from memory.

No one was going to pass this final unless the memory they were drawing upon was photographic. Seeing as that no one in class possessed this unusual genetic trait, properly termed as Eidetic Imagery (which according to Scientific American is prevalent in only 2% of pre-adolescents but nearly non-existent in adults) -- no one passed the final.

Ergo, my "A" I'd earned all semester was averaged with my final's grade of "F", and I came out of the class with a "C". I later came to find out that the instructor for this class touted herself as having the most difficult Lit class in all the College, and was not happy with the amount of "A's" that had been earned that semester. So, to keep her reputation as a real GPA buster, she sprang this impossible test on a class that really should have been an outstanding reflection of her ability to teach. I learned quickly in my short time within the academic system that the ego on many academic professionals was often tied to their ability to lord their knowledge over others, and I had no time for this no-win game created by that type of emotionally insecure minutia. College was insufferable enough without having to wade through the personal issues of these weirdoes.

Besides, I always thought this Lit professor was bat-crap crazy anyway. Not only would she only address only the left half of the class – I mean, ONLY address, as if we on the right half were completely invisible and she was teaching to a cigar-shaped room, but she'd pace and prattle on and on while her slip would worm it's way out from beneath her skirt, ending every class at least seven inches below the hem -- the professor none the wiser that her undies were flapping in the breeze. That type of oblivion takes a certain self-absorption that was well and truly above my pay grade. It fascinated me. Thus, I'd check in on her throughout the day, sneaking a glance through the narrow window on the door as I passed to my next class. And, as expected, there she would be, prattling on and on to the left half of the room three hours later, that poor neglected slip still not adjusted. By noon, the undies would be dangling off of her hips, a white flag limply waving mid-shin as her fashion sense declared defeat, having lost the battle with the slick rubber sides of some god-forsaken girdle left over from Jackie O's stay at the White House. After her lunch, I'd check through the window, and everyday the slip would have been tucked back up where it belongs -- no doubt a fortunate side-effect from her finally using the restroom rather than an intentional corrective choice.

Her behavior would have made more sense if she were an Extraterrestrial. As it stands, I'm still bitter and I want my "A" back, lest I pen some dry piece of garbage in protest for inclusion within her torturous bible-thin-paged text book, aptly entitled: "Students in the Hands of an Angry Grad".

Anyway.

Jake and I would get out of class and drown our sorrows in a good view, heading up to the sandstone cliffs that border our hometown on the north side – the Rimrocks. We spent a lot of time there growing up, as did most Billings-ites. It was the go-to place to unwind, and the view was spectacular. On a clear day, we could see 100 miles in every direction, from the Beartooth Rockies in the west to the Pryor Mountains in the south. Atop the Beartooth Rockies was home of the infamous Hell-Roarin' Plateau at 11,000 feet, created by the incomprehensible weight of Ice Age Glaciers shaving off the top of an entire mountain range. The Pryor Mountains to the south, the northern extension of the Bighorn Mountain Range, was home of the prehistoric

80 foot wide Medicine Wheel, a holy site constructed by ancient Native Americans around 800 years ago.

The Pryor Mountains are known as the home of what the Crow Indian Tribe call *Awwakkulé,* or "The Little People", a mystical group of ferocious dwarf-like creatures with no neck and sharp canine-like teeth. The Crow believe that petroglyphs carved on the mountain rocks to be the work of The Little People, and as such, they consider the mountains sacred

The legend of The Little People is common amongst Native American tribes with accounts of the creatures dating as far back as 9,000 years. In every story, these beings possess super-human strength and supernatural weaponry – very sharp arrows which could effectively strike from unusually far distances. Even famed western explorers Lewis and Clark wrote of The Little People in 1804 after staying with the Sioux tribe in what is now South Dakota, traveling with the Sioux up the Missouri River to see "the mountain of the Little People". Meriwether Lewis documented a description of The Little People in his journal as devils (originally written as "deavals") standing about 18 inches high with extremely large heads. Lewis went on to report that three local Native American tribes feared the Little People so much that they would not go near their area, as The Little People were hyper aware of anyone trespassing in their territory, and didn't blink at killing intruders.

The Little People could appear and disappear in an instant. Said to be highly carnivorous, the Crow lore spoke of how The Little People tapped their superhuman strength to pull a felled Elk by simply throwing the creature's head over their shoulder, spurring the saying "strong as a dwarf". The Crow would leave offerings to the Little People in order to gain safe passage through the mountains, as The Little People were known to steal children and tobacco, and to eat the hearts from horses. The Little People were also said to possess the ability to see into the future, blessing the famed Crow Chief, Plenty Coup, with visions of how to survive both the arrival of the white man and the death of the Plains Indian lifestyle.

Let's see -- big heads, short stance, the ability to instantly disappear, powerful weapons that could shoot farther than anything ever encountered, Psychic and Telepathic abilities, cutting organs out of livestock  – by modern standards, The Little People could make an appearance on the X-Files as the Zeta Reticuli Grey aliens that Fox Mulder was chasing.

However, I myself have happened upon energetic pockets in the Bighorn Canyon as well as The Pryor Mountains where The Little

People still congregate, and as much as I'd love to label them as ET's, they are in fact inter-dimensional Elementals – nature's "middle-management" -- that guard wide-open vortex points in the mountains. They're more akin to Trolls, Fey (fairies), or -- yes – Bigfoot, which is also not only real, but an inter-dimensional. Elementals are often mistaken as Demons due to their less-than-appealing appearance and nasty temperament, which, though intolerant to the point of violence when encountering human stupidity – is hardly "evil". All the same, I can tell you that the Plains Indians have it right: The Little People aren't to be messed with.

Every child who grows up in Montana knows the lore of The Little People and how to stay out of their way. Which was why in all of our time growing up and enjoying the outdoors, Jake and I stayed to safe pastures, such the Rimrocks that overlooked town. Though the Pryor Mountains were ceremonial for the Crow, the Rimrocks were ceremonial for the rest of us chickens. It was the place we all went to reflect -- or, to make out while the city lights twinkled below. But in the case of me and my childhood friend Jake – the night I'm about to recount was definitely an issue of reflection.

One summer after I graduated high school and before I was to be dispersed to Arizona (I was two years ahead of Jake in school), we picked up pal our "Susan" to have one last powwow atop the get-away plateau known as The Rims. We were all lying on the hood of Jake's car, shoulder to shoulder, staring at the stars in the night sky. I don't remember what we were talking about -- something melancholy no doubt, as we were teenagers and the thought of our long-time group being disbanded was the first life lesson in separation from those who buffer you from the world – when our conversation began to trail off.

We were all witnessing the same thing, high up in the night sky, right above the city.

"Are you seeing this, Jake?" I said.

"Yes," he answered in his signature stoic way.

"What the hell…?" was Susan's offering to the conversation.

As we'd spent hours talking, we had all been staring at the same general area of the sky, right above our heads. The sky was full of stars whose only movement was an occasional twinkling. Suddenly, three of these stars broke their stasis in the night sky and began heading toward one another, as if on a slow and deliberate collision course. This was enough to interrupt our conversation, as we all knew that stars don't move, and satellites don't sit still for hours. It was this bizarre sight --

three "stars" breaking their pattern in the night sky to head toward one another -- that cut our conversation short.

The "stars" came into close proximity to form a large triangle. Moments later, a bright oval-shaped object came tearing straight up the center of the sky and over our heads, running south to north. It wasn't as blazingly fast as a shooting star, but was much too fast to be a satellite, clearing the horizon south to north in around five or six seconds. And, it was much too big to be a satellite – this thing was obviously above the atmosphere judging by its star-like glow that was shared by the other celestial bodies around it – however, it was enormous, being the size of my pinky-finger nail, even from such a distance. The oval-shaped object whisked directly past the triangle of "repositioned stars" and was swallowed by the earth's curve on the northern horizon. Seconds later, the triangle of stars swiveled, so the "point" was facing the direction that the oval had just disappeared, and ZIP – the entire triangle, moving as one body, shot off after the oval -- from a dead stand-still.

There was dead silence on the hood of Jake's car, finally broken by an articulate Susan:

"What the hell."

It made sense that the UFO's headed north, as up north outside of Great Falls was Malmstrom Air Force Base. Barely over 177 miles from Billings, Malmstrom AFB is one of the most noted locations in the country for an encounter with a UFO, as documented by the Air Force itself. This again makes sense when one is made aware that the great open expanse of unpopulated Montana land is not only home to chirping Meadowlarks and Prairie Dogs, but is actually chock full of intercontinental nuclear missile silos. (Because nothing says Mother Nature like a W56 nuclear warhead and 1.5 megatons of TNT.)

In March of 1967, a UFO was reported by the Air Force to have not only hovered over the Minuteman Strategic missiles at the Echo LLC site, part of Malmstrom AFB, but to have disabled the entire arsenal's power and guidance systems for all 50 missiles. Not a power outage base wide, mind you, just the missiles registering as "no-go" -- non-operational due to a Guidance and System (G & S) fault that could not be explained. That same morning, 20 miles away outside of Roy, Montana at a Minuteman Strategic missile portal known as Oscar-Flight LLC, the exact same thing happened with their entire arsenal of 50 missiles, only their account of the UFO was more detailed: A red-glowing saucer shape that hovered silently at the front gate. An airman who had approached the UFO was injured and rushed for medical attention.

Both missile locations, and both plots of missiles, were rendered completely useless for an entire day. This was a huge and terrifying threat to national security, as in 1967, the United States was in the throws of the Vietnam War – only one year away from its peak with the Tet Offensive of 1968 – as well as in the height of the Cold War with the Soviet Union, and only 5 years clear of 1962's nail-biting Cuban Missile Crisis. Frantic teams of engineers including Boeing professionals were unable to find cause for the G & S fault at both missile locations, and concluded the only thing capable of causing such a failure would be an enormous EMF (Electro Magnetic Field) pulse – something that back in the day could not have been produced without an outrageous amount of heavy equipment.

Yep, Montana was well-acquainted with UFO's. From airmen to farmers to businessmen caught unaware on the long drive from Missoula to Butte, to three teenagers musing about the future, Montanans were privy to what lurked above in the skies. That night while saying goodbye to my high school days, along with Jake and Sharon, I had my first official encounter with OffWorlders -- the "Little People" of the skies.

Little did I know that it was not going to be my last.

# 7
# ALIENS, ABDUCTIONS, AND IMPLANTS -- OH MY!
## WHERE: MY CHILDHOOD HOME / MY NORTHWEST HOME
## LOCATION: BILLINGS, MONTANA / SEATTLE, WA

*Part i - Abduction*

What do sleeping in the basement, distorted shadows on the ceiling, and complete paralysis have in common? Well, absolutely nothing -- unless you're talking Alien abduction.

In 1990, I was back in Montana from Arizona. I had quit college, only to end up attending Eastern Montana College anyway. That was a short-lived decision as well, but in the interim I moved in with my parents; back into my childhood bedroom in the basement. Upon moving home from Arizona, I made a few changes to the room – the most notable being that I swapped my waterbed in favor of a single twin mattress for more space, to create a "studio apartment" feel. On one side of the room was my keyboard and MIDI set-up bought for me by my Grandpa while I was in Arizona to use in music production. Next to the keyboard was my stereo – or rather, my parent's old stereo, with Bose speakers and a genuine Marantz tube receiver. Against the other wall was the new twin mattress and lots of floor space in between to move around.

My best friend "Pearl" and I had rolled in late from being out somewhere, and decided that it was best just to go to sleep. Pearl didn't want to drive home, and I didn't blame her so I invited her to scrunch into the little single bed with me. Well, neither Pearl nor I had any problem bunking together in a tight space as we'd been best friends since fourth grade and were familiar bunk mates. It also helped that we were both stick skinny little things back in our very early twenties. Her size two and my size four had plenty of room in the single bed.

Pearl was snuggled up on the side of the bed that was pushed against the wall, and I was on the side that opened to the room. I turned out the light and crawled into bed, the soft blue display light from the Marantz receiver casting a soft glow everywhere. It was nice to have the room lit with a "night light" of sorts; that room had always been too dark at night.

It takes me awhile to fall asleep and it always has. As a small child, I never wanted to go to sleep, because while my parents would be sawing logs in the other room, there I'd be-- awake, in the dark, by myself -- left with whatever else was lurking around. I have forever envied those who can place their head on a pillow and pass right out. What a gift that would be. Just because one wishes to sleep does not mean that one's Sixth Sense is on board. And just as we have to close our eyes to inspire our brain to down-shift into REM, those of us who were born with a few extra receivers in the bandwidth must find ways to close all of our eyes.

For me, finding ways to get to sleep has been an ongoing process, weeding out incoming Psychic transmission after energetic transmission – trying to find a lull in the never-ending surf of information, events, and emotions crashing constantly against my own shoreline, 24 hours a day, seven days a week, 365 days a year – year after year. On a non-psychotic level, I can somewhat relate with the constant onslaught endured by those who suffer with schizophrenia. Of course, no little voices are telling me to kill myself or kill others. I do, however, occasionally hear voices, but I'm also a Medium, and those voices are attached to disembodied people who are usually asking for my help. Not asking me to kill the President.

While I'm awake, I don't notice the influx of information nearly as much, as not only am I built to receive all that information so it's just part of my day, but the noise and pace of the day take precedent. Yet when I lay me down to sleep, the waterfall of information is much more noticeable -- predictions of world events, the neighbor's anxiety as he pores over bills, the outcome of projects I've got rolling, a satellite passing overhead pinging too loudly and grabbing my attention, any geothermal movement deep in the earth, bizarre stuff coming out of Washington D.C. – the list is truly endless. For the most part, I've learned to ignore it and treat it as white noise in the background of my consciousness. Yet sometimes even that doesn't work. When I first moved to Los Angeles in 2002, I was unprepared for the amount of energy one must process while living amidst a metropolitan area that includes 30 million people. For the first three years, I stared a hole through my ceiling every night, feeling as if my head was in a bee hive. I've gotten better over the years at tuning out that constant and pulsing HUM that creates the energetic undercurrent in the City of Angels. But I still have my nights where I lay there staring at the ceiling, slowly digging myself a trench within my own subconscious in which to duck out of the fray, until my body follows suit.

This can take awhile, so I've always had an easier time sleeping if I mentally wear myself out prior to going to bed. Though the sixth sense is spiritual, I'm in a physical body, and sometimes, all meditation and Namaste aside – you just have to punt. When worst comes to worst, run the car out of gas, and you will have to pull over. Wearing myself out – and I mean that in a healthy way -- can be achieved through any creative endeavor. Writing, music, performance and design work are terrific in channeling all of that energy coming in from the ethers. Another way to move through all that energy is by spending a day out in nature or with some physical exertion. If that doesn't work or I'm in a pinch, sometimes taking a Benadryl or sipping a glass of wine will help -- but never at once. I'm not Marilyn Monroe. Besides, occasional sleep aids or alcohol aren't that effective because they don't really fix the issue since it's not physiological, but they will sometimes distract me from the noise that's ongoing. Reading will eventually do the trick, if I have an hour or two. However, my best sleep is above 5,000 feet in the middle of nowhere after I've exerted myself greatly in some wonderful way, where the only thing pulsing is the earth and the crickets – two tones and two energies, on the deliciously opposite end of the spectrum. Whatever it takes, falling asleep easily has never been my forte. When I die, I plan on sleeping a lot in heaven -- a peaceful, quiet, perfect sleep, sprawled out in the middle of my very own cloud.

That night back in Montana, I certainly didn't have a cloud on which to sleep. Nor was I in the middle of nowhere. In fact, Pearl and I hadn't partaken in anything out of the ordinary that day, clouds or otherwise, so my ol' noggin hadn't been run around the corral a time or two. As was her usual M.O., Pearl zonked out, and as was my usual M.O. -- I didn't.

We were both lying quietly on our backs in the bed, Pearl's shoulder crunched up against mine in the twin bed. I had my arms crossed over my chest – not meaning to look like a mummy, but it was the best place to put my arms due to the limited space. I was observing the peaceful cast of soft light created by the Marantz receiver's blue glow. The room felt better once the waterbed was removed, and the sound of Pearl's sleep breathing was a hopeful indication that perhaps within the next half hour, even I had the potential of joining her in the Land of Nod.

All of a sudden, out of nowhere on the ceiling above the bed, appeared this beautiful yellow ripple of light. It looked exactly like the reflections of water made by indoor pools on the gymnasium roof above. It was a most calming yellowish ripple that danced across a small area of the bedroom ceiling, almost like wind blowing across waves, or light yellow feathers glowing softly as they were puffed across the roof. I was instantly infused with an enormous sense of deep peace. Such a sense flowed through my veins that I didn't even question the fact that this very out-of-place golden yellow reflection was dancing on my ceiling. In fact, this beautiful lilting golden ripple had a hypnotic quality lulled me into simply staring, in full marvel of this soft-colored illuminated dance of light.

It's very important to point out here that I, in no way, was asleep. I was nowhere close to asleep. In fact, I was in the process of actively envying the sleep that Pearl seemed to be getting.

The ripple began to pick up, as if the reflection on the gymnasium ceiling reflected wind blowing across the pool. As the dance of light escalated, and I fell deeper into this hypnotic bliss, I could hear a noise, off to my right – directly where the open floor would be. It was a very distant sound, as if far, far off, echoing down a tunnel. It was a mechanical sound, like an enormous generator or engine, metal clanking against metal – Ca-CHINK Ca-CHUNK, Ca-CHINK Ca-CHUNK – slowly coming closer, as if through the floor.

Again, this is not striking me as odd, because I am far to mesmerized by this dance of rippling lights on the ceiling whose overwhelming effect caused me to feel as if nothing in the world was wrong with this picture. Like a morphine drip straight into my neck, those lights made absolutely everything blissful and okay. It was a euphoric feeling that inspired me not to look away from these rippling reflections.

Pearl was still dead asleep next to me, and didn't seem to respond to the metallic Ca-CHINK Ca-CHUNK that was slowly coming closer – as if surfacing right under the shag carpet in the middle of the room.

As I lay transfixed by these yellow ripples on the ceiling, I saw a most unusual object approach, hovering about four feet above me, carefully moving over the foot of my bed. It looked like a three foot wide by five foot long translucent gray rectangle – like a cross between a dense mist and a piece of matte gray cellophane. I could see through it and it cast a gray tone to everything on the other side of it, in the same way that looking through the lenses of sunglasses will color-taint the overall view. This strange, thin, floating rectangle continued to cruise up past my knees, past my hips, past my chest, until it was floating directly above me, and then it stopped.

The dancing yellow light above, which was now rippling on the ceiling quite quickly, appeared gray through this barrier. Again, none of this was striking me as odd, as I was still basking in this ridiculously euphoric feeling of peace instilled in me by these reflective lights. It was as though something had jumped the critical thinking circuit in my brain, and my "What the hell?" response was replaced with, "There's nothing to fear. This is normal." One would think that, in and of itself, would have been enough to ignite red flags all up and down the corridors of my conscious mind. Yet my conscious mind was dosed up on bliss. Danielle wasn't there anymore, Mrs. Torrence. I've never felt anything like it, before or since. The closest thing with which I'm able to draw a likeness is the mellow haze brought on by pain-killing narcotics. But this sensation really put a bucket of Oxycodone to shame.

The strange see-through gray rectangle, which had been hovering above, began to lower itself down upon me, as if a magician was carefully lowering his magic scarf as part of a trick. Off to the side of the bed, the metallic Ca-CHINK Ca-CHUNK was growing closer, up through the floor. I could now detect what sounded like great steam pressure, releasing with every rotation of this huge metallic engine. As this sound came closer, it reminded me somewhat of the factory sound effect in Billy Joel's song "Allentown". And, the clink-clank, coupled with the steam pressure sound, made me very aware that whatever was creating this sound had to have been enormous, heavy, and housed in an equally enormous – in fact, cavernous – space, judging by the echo.

Still, Pearl slept on.

Again, was I alarmed that here in my room was not only some bizarre floating see-through thing accompanying dancing ripples on the ceiling, but also the Allentown sound effect coming from the concrete basement floor? Not in the slightest. I was too busy being mystified by this translucent rectangle. As it approached closer to my face, my natural reaction was to pull my head back. And this is where the story really goes down the rabbit hole.

I pulled my face backward, all right, yet my body stayed exactly where it was. Let me repeat that: *I* moved. My *body* did not. My consciousness was completely separate from my body. I was clear to the back of my own head, on the inside, "looking up" through my eyes – a view which looked exactly like holding a Halloween mask six inches from your face and staring through the eye holes. I could see this gray triangle settle and drape over the eyes holes, and I realized it was lying on my face, but I could not feel it. Staring up through the eyeholes in the mask of my own face from the back of my head, everything in on the ceiling appear darker one the gray rectangle was draped – again, like putting on a pair of smoke-gray sunglasses.

All of a sudden I was acutely aware that me – who I really was, my spirit -- and my body, were no longer hooked up together. And, as such, I couldn't move. I mean, not just "not moving", but the fact was, my body might as well have been a petrified hunk of iron. This whole sensation gave a new meaning to "dead weight". It wasn't that I couldn't move. It was that the whole idea of movement was completely ridiculous. I was painfully aware of how incredibly heavy the human body was – how much energy it took to propel this sack of water and organs, from day to day. Now, it was nothing more than a paralyzed log of flesh concrete, frozen just as I had laid it down, my hands crossed over my chest like some demented mummy. There I was, floating inside myself, free from that everyday weight, like floating in my own sarcophagus.

Was I terrified? Was I spun into a state of utter hysteria, trapped inside of myself? Of course not. I was high as a kite on some supernatural narcotic. Instead, the fact that I could move about freely in my own body gave me a warm sense of security. I thought specifically: "Aha! They can't get me in here."

Let's just take a moment to analyze this realization while not under the influence of some other-wordly whoopee juice, shall we? Who in the heck is "we", and why did I jump right to the assumption that "they" were coming to "get me"? None of that occurred to me at the time.

And Pearl? Out like a light.

Once the floating rectangle had been lowered onto me, draping like some translucent shroud -- that's when the sound of an enormous pressure release burst into the room, and the floor opened up. That's right, what would have been the floor space to my right, suddenly opened, like a hatch with two sliding sides. I say "hatch" because though I couldn't turn my head to see the floor, I could still see the ceiling. And on the ceiling, accompanied by what you'd think of a classic "Star Wars" pressurized hatch-opening sound, a brilliantly yellowish light – obviously shining through the doorway that had appeared in the floor -- formed a skinny line that kept widening and widening. As the hatch doors widened, a bright yellow square grew on the ceiling.

Now that the "floor hatch" was open, the metallic Ca-CHINK Ca-CHUNK Ca-CHINK Ca-CHUNK flooded the room, deafening at this point. For the very first time, I started to feel something other than euphoria. I started to feel…anxious. Not anxious that there was an intra-dimensional hatch in my room – that blatant and obvious realization hadn't quite drilled its way through the hypnotic haze with which I'd been doused. The anxiety came on because the grinding metal sound was so close. It was no longer the dancing reflections of light on the ceiling. It was no longer a floating mist-blanket being lowered gently. It was an unnerving and huge racket – and in my room. I wanted to turn my head to see what was opening in my floor, but again – I couldn't. My head and neck were reduced to a monolith of granite, dead on the pillow.

Something was coming -- though the floor. On the ceiling above me, movement; the shadow of a figure appeared… then two, then three. Something was coming into my room.

The shadows bobbed back and forth as they walked, indicating that they weren't very tall. They all seemed to come around a corner and turn up a ramp or walkway of some kind to spill into my room. Their shadows were at first huge and blurry on the ceiling, backlit from whatever was creating this bright yellow cast up through the floor. As they moved farther up the "ramp", their shadows grew smaller. I was aware that they were moving away from this light source and into my room because of the way their shadows morphed in size on the ceiling. I was instantly drawn back to being a child, playing with my Grandpa's flashlight in a dark room. If I held my hand close to the light, the shadow on the wall would appear big, distorted, and blurry. The farther my hand was moved away from the light, closer to the wall, the more defined the shadow on the wall appeared, to finally resemble a hand. This exact same principle was at play, so I knew that whatever was coming, they were moving away from the light source, and into my room.

The figures emerged "out" of the floor and turned right – again, I could not turn my head, but I could see their shadows turning on the ceiling. When they turned, I caught a profile of these creatures – and that's when whatever last bit of euphoric haze in my consciousness was expunged from my system by a rush of good old fashioned adrenaline.

These creatures seemed to have long, hooked "noses", like the Muppet Gonzo. In all fairness, I couldn't turn my head to look at them, so maybe this "hooked nose" was some sort of helmet, or apparatus of some kind. But it really did look like a nose from the angle of the shadow.

The creatures bobbed back and forth as they lined up next to my side of the bed. Immediately, my mind went to Evil Trolls, or maybe Demons. This seemed to make the most sense since they came out of the floor in a glowing yellowish haze – hey, that could be the reflection of hell fire, right? – and it certainly would explain that terrible metallic grinding sound. Maybe chains? And the steam sound could make sense, because maybe hell was hot? My mind was spinning, trying to make sense of the whole thing. I had no idea what in the heck these things were, and my Evangelical Christian background didn't provide many templates for Otherworldly Phenomenon outside of Angels or Demons. These definitely weren't Angels.

They weren't Demons either, and something deep inside of me knew this. However, I had an instant fear of these creatures the minute I saw their shadows. Actually, I wasn't as much afraid of them, to be perfectly honest – I was more afraid of the fact that they were going to take me somewhere that I didn't want to go. Again, looking back – how would I know that? But I did, and for the first time in the evening – I thought about how all of this would affect Pearl.

My God, I had Troll Demons lined up by the bed, this screaming metallic Ca-CHINK Ca-CHUNK blowing noise all over the place, and Pearl was dead to the world as if under anesthesia. Why wasn't she waking up? Who could sleep through this onslaught of light and sound? My body was absolutely useless, and to say I couldn't move is an understatement. My consciousness had been completely separated from my physical being. The battery had been taken out of the car.

That's when I figured it out. In a terrifying split second, I realized exactly what had been happening: Like a charging bull elephant taken down on the plains of the Serengeti -- I had been shot with an Ethereal Elephant Dart.

Whatever these things were, they had an ingenious method of disabling someone much bigger than they were. Somehow, these lights on the ceiling stimulated a certain part of the human brain to create the illusion of peaceful sedation. While this peace was settling, the other half of this effect was to "short circuit" our awareness, like being hypnotized and told that you're made of stone. These hypnotic lights separated mind from body. In a more primitive race like Humankind, who still believes that we are our body (not having transcended the concept of a mind-body union) – that's like taking the tires off of a car and leaving the metal frame up on blocks. If a person didn't have a very decent command of that fact that they were indeed a spiritual being living a physical existence – that there were two pieces of the puzzle that made up their consciousness, not one -- they would simply lay in paralyzed terror with the feeling of being trapped. I, however, had a very different awareness.

Thanks to my earlier experience with the floating gray rectangular veil, I was very aware that I was separate from my body. *I* could move, but my body could not. Those are two different animals. And as these weird beings lined up next to my bed, this all-encompassing panic of adrenaline flooded me – not as much for me, but for the clueless Pearl, laying there passed out. She was completely unaware that something had crawled out of the depths of hell and was planning to drag me, and maybe her, off to some frightening place somewhere. I had to snap out of this. I had to do something.

It was then that I took everything I had to muster – and I mean EVERY bit of focus I had -- and I said to myself, over and over again, in only that panicked way a person can when they realize they've run out of time.

CONNECT. CONNECT. CONNECT UP WITH YOURSELF!

It was a Herculean effort. I had a visual image of some large cable at the base of my brain, right at my spine, twisting into place to connect my head with the rest of my body. In one desperate and gigantic internal push, I connected my spiritual consciousness with my body – and man, was my body HEAVY. Against the incomprehensively dragging weight of gravity and my own physical being, I pulled my crossed arms from my chest and threw them underneath me -- thrusting myself up onto my elbows. My head hung backward, a dead sack of sand, yet unmovable. Now that my consciousness was "forward" again, I was looking directly out of my eyes instead of looking through holes in a mask from the back of my head, As such, I had peripheral vision in addition to watching the shadows on the ceiling.

Right next to my bed, inches from me, were three figures, each about three feet high. They were a peachy color, or appeared that way from the yellowish light coming through the floor. They had rounded bulbous heads and very small bodies, and I could not make out any specific facial features. In fact, they didn't look at all like their shadows. And that's when I realized that how I interpreted the shadows may have been directly affected by the hypnotic drug-like affect imposed by the rippling lights overhead. The lights were designed to keep me paralyzed, either physically, or in fear of what I would fear the most. My consciousness went right to Demons.

These guys were good.

The next sequence of events happened very quickly: As I thrust up on my elbows, the gray rectangle that had once shrouded me shot straight off into the air, repelled by my movement. As if choreographed, these three figures took a quick step backward in unison with the rectangle. They were incredibly startled. I could feel them. They were somehow connected to this gray rectangle in consciousness, and with each other. They moved as one body and they all were extremely surprised that I moved. I can't say they were frightened – these beings didn't have that type of emotionality. But they were shocked, in an analytical sort of way. Their puzzlement was very sincere. My whole sitting-up-thing was well and truly out of their paradigm.

Apparently, I wasn't supposed to be able to do what I did. They had no protocol for that.

I was still in sync with these beings, and for those few moments, I understood that without the ability to bypass our consciousness using their Hypnotic Hi-Ball, we posed these beings great physical threat. We were much larger and much physically stronger. And, we were much more impulsive. Without sedation, they saw us as incredibly violent – and incredibly dangerous.

Mission aborted.

The three figures immediately scurried back down the "ramp" – I couldn't turn my head yet but in my periphery I could see what looked like some sort of square hole in the floor with light flooding through. It was indeed some sort of inter-dimensional "hatch" exploding up through my basement carpet. I watched their shadows on the ceiling zipping back down the walkway from which they'd come, the shadows growing more and more blurry as they scurried off into the depths of wherever it was they came from.

The sound of the closing pressurized hatch burst into the room. I watched on the ceiling as the two hatch doors slid together, narrowing the yellow square until the light was pinched into a bright line – then nothing. The deafening mechanical Ca-CHINK Ca-CHUNK and all its pounding steam was muffled once again beneath the doors below. Slowly, just as it had arrived, the sound moved away, echoing down what sounded like a long passageway. Tiny remnants of the feathery yellow reflective lights on the ceiling faded in tandem with the sound trailing off into the far distance. Ca-CHINK Ca-CHUNK, Ca-CHINK Ca-CHUNK…

Finally, it was just me the quiet blue glow of the Marantz receiver.

I was still propped up on my elbows, and still couldn't move. I felt so heavy. I was acutely aware of gravity for the first time in my life. I had no idea the human body weighed so much. Slowly, eventually, I gained one bit of mobility, then another, as I "thawed out" from whatever stasis I'd been thrust into. I was finally able to turn my head. I looked at the clock. It was 2:16 a.m. Later, I could raise my head. By the time I could move enough to sit up, it was after 2:30 a.m. My neck was screaming in pain from having been hyper-extended backwards by the weight of my own noggin for such a long time. Clearly, I hadn't been dreaming. It doesn't take 20 minutes to wake from a dream.

Yet still -- Pearl slept on.

The next day I said nothing about the event to Pearl. What was I going to say? I had no idea what had happened either. I asked her how she slept. She said she had weird dreams. When I asked her about the content of her dreams, she told me that she couldn't recall. Something about hiding from ghosts, or monsters, but she couldn't remember – just that they were really weird.

I bet they were.

*Part ii ~ Siriusly, Aliens? I'm Sirius!*

Of all my paranormal experiences, that bizarre night in my childhood bedroom was the most complicated to understand. Ghosts are spirits of people. They are predictable to a degree, as are human beings. Demons are predictable as well, as they despise Light and have a very specific way of approaching humanity. Both Demons and Humankind have one thing in common: emotional responses, even though Demonic "emotionality" tips more toward the sociopathic and narcissistic side of the scale. But still, it's something. You can feel them. These beings, however, were something all-together different – not one lick of emotionality present. And if you locked into one being's consciousness, you locked into them all.

It took me years of research, pulling information out from beneath rocks, so to speak, until I was able to understand what had occurred with me that night. I came to find out that people who make claims of abduction by Aliens, or Extra Terrestrials – what I call OffWorlders – recall these very same symptoms that I'd experienced: paralysis, beings appearing out of nowhere, bright lights, sounds. Even Pearl's super-human ability to stay asleep in the midst of such mayhem was cited, with abductees claiming that their spouses would remain dead asleep next to them, trance-like, unaware of all the activity in the room. That made sense to me. If these beings could disconnect human consciousness from the body with a frequency of light, they could surely knock someone out and keep them out.

In my instance, it seemed as though the abduction didn't go as planned. However, I read quite a bit about time distortion with Alien Abductees -- how people who had been abducted were suddenly put back where they were taken from, thinking that they had never left and no time had passed, when in fact they were taken somewhere else for an extended length of time. It could have been possible that what I thought was me sitting up, thwarting an abduction, was actually me being placed back into the room, after the abduction. However, I truly don't believe this was my case, as thanks to my own Sixth Sense abilities, I could feel and sense these entities – and my whole "sitting up" thing really, really wasn't in their plan.

I did realize in retrospect that these beings – at least, the OffWorlders that were dealing with me -- were able to bend space and time, and be in two places at once. My room never went anywhere, and they never had a "ship" that came to me through the floor. Instead, these beings had the ability to "fold space", then poke a hole in it, and walk through. The Ca-CHINK Ca-CHUNK mechanical sound was no doubt created by whatever apparatus was able to bend time and keep a wormhole open, and what I interpreted as a "steam", I've come to find out, was likely the sound of a Electromagnetic pressure being released as a temporal doorway was held open, between two points in the universe. I'm sure there was actually a hatch, from one pressure point in the universe to the next – like the locks in the Panama Canal.

Interdimensional travel and OffWorlders go hand in hand. If you'd like a more recent example of this technology, Google "Norway Spiral", a temporal event that occurred on December 9th, 2009, in the skies above Skjervoy, Norway. This event was caught on video by thousands of smart phone users as well as documented on and flip cams and local news cameras. It looks faked, like someone's computer graphics projects in college -- but it's not. In fact, another spiral just like the one that appeared in Norway crested in the sky above China on October 7th, 1983.

In the videos you'll be able to note that as the spiral opens a "hole" in space high in the night sky, the "blackness" of the hole is far blacker than the dark of night surrounding the hole. That's because the vacuum of space is actually "darker" than the dark of night as represented in our earth's atmosphere. Even though the sun has set on earth, tiny particles of moisture and matter trapped in our dense atmosphere reflect tiny bits of light. In space, nothing is trapped anywhere to reflect anything, and there's a lot more…well, space. Thus its namesake. So it's just a lot darker.

Anyway, as the Norway Spiral twirls, opening up a "hole" in space – think of it like a temporal door jam – a curly blue light corkscrews from the center of the door jam, and extends to the ground. That's actually like an enormous escalator extending from the wormhole to the earth.

After seeing this phenomenon all over the internet, it's easy to understand why a spiral is the most ancient and common symbol in archeology, transcending time periods, world cultures, and geographic regions. Obviously, this wasn't The Norway Spiral's first appearance. 10,000 year old spirals are found carved into cave walls as well as etched into pillars at St. John the Divine Cathedral in New York City, right under a lamb (Lamb of God), some ancient mummies, and a child being birthed. Sidebar: The mere fact that a birthing child pushing its way through a stylized vagina was chosen to be carved into a major Catholic Cathedral is much more wonky to me than a Stargate, or ET's. For a religion that wishes to encourage having a family, depicting the vaginal stretch around a baby's cranium is probably not the way to do it. Ouch. Thanks be to God.

Speaking of God, this blue Norway Spiral in the sky matches up with two pre-Columbian Hopi prophecies. The first contains a series of final warnings foretelling of a "The Great Purification of the World by Fire." According to tribal elders, this purification could be fire upon the earth *or* fire of the spirit to bring change. In the four corners of Arizona, ancient glyphs are carved into the Hopi Prophecy Rock and depict two timelines: One where mankind continues onward in folly and greed, destroyed by a jagged cork screw spiral coming down from the sky; the other timeline depicts Humankind righting itself to return to the equitable circle of life, being spared death from the sky.

The second Hopi Prophecy states: "When the Blue Star Kachina makes its appearance in the heavens, the Fifth World will emerge". This 5th World is said to be the Day of Purification by Fire, arriving when the Saquasohuh (Blue Star) Kachina removes its mask and dances. The "Blue Star Kachina" is the Hopi name for the famed star Sirius, located in the constellation Canis Major ("The Big Dog") – ironically, the same star that the Egyptians, Sumerians and many ancient cultures held dear in their worship of ancient signs and mystic ET messengers. The Dogon, an African tribe located in what's now the Mali Republic, have documented in their ancient history the fact that Sirius is a binary star system – knowledge they could never have obtained without the use of a modern telescope. The Dogon's lore of the 50-year orbit of Sirius B around Sirius A is absolutely accurate. The tribe claimed the "sacred knowledge" was given to them by a race of ET's that they considered to be gods visiting Earth from the Sirius star system itself. Egyptians associated Sirius with the god Osiris, and of course, there's the whole issue of the Queen's chamber in the Great Pyramid of Giza containing a "window shaft" that is directly lined up with the star since they felt it to be the soul of Isis. Sirius is even believed by many to be the famed "Star of Bethlehem" that led Wise Men from the East to the Birthplace of Jesus Christ. Granted, one could argue that Sirius gets all this attention because it was – and still is -- the brightest fixed star in the sky. But seeing as that Sirius weighs-in so mystically heavy, time and time again, – maybe 10,000 years of Human culture was onto something that deserves a mention in this chapter.

Sirius connection or not, The Norway Spiral also appeared in the sky at a rather auspicious time— the night before President Barack Obama was scheduled to give his Nobel Prize acceptance speech in Oslo, Norway, 758 miles away. The Norway Spiral was supposedly debunked immediately as an experimental Russian missile that cork-screwed off course. The problem with that missile story is three-fold: 1) If indeed a stray experimental Russian missile went wild over Norway and blew up into a crazy pinwheel rotating in space unlike anything ever seen, it would be unlikely that the United States would allow our Commander In Chief  to be dispatched into such an unsecure area, plus 2) the off-course missile-corkscrew theory doesn't really work out because the corkscrew came FROM the center of the black hole that opened in the center of The Norway Spiral, and the corkscrew of light unfurled TOWARD the earth, not the other way around, and finally 3) The Russians debunked any story of a stray missile, saying they never did have a missile misfire that night, especially over Norway. (Apparently, they didn't get the memo.)

So, obviously, just like a family waiting at the train station, the world's leaders were expecting the spiral. Perhaps along with being attended by some of the world' most influential leaders, maybe our OffWorld friends were arriving in time to attend Barack Obama's Nobel Peace Prize speech? Or perhaps, more likely, The President needed to be present in Norway, along with many of the world's leading scientists, to greet a delegation of our OffWorld friends who could only arrive when the Earth's geomagnetic properties allowed the wormhole to open? The latter makes a touch more sense, if we factor in two last pieces missing from the puzzle.

Stay with me here – this gets good:

It just so happened that the Norway Spiral's appearance in the sky occurred at the same time that HAARP (High Frequency Active Auroral Research Program) and the LHC (Large Hadron Collider) -- two heavy-hitting fringe physics installments -- were both conducting tests. What do these science experiments have to do with our X-Files adjacent story, you may ask? Well, the LHC deals with attempting to fuse atomic particles, which has to do with wormholes, and HAARP deals with solar-terrestrial physics, which has to do with the Earth's upper atmosphere.

Considering The Norway Spiral is a wormhole that rotated in the upper atmosphere, we may have a winner.

HAARP is operated on a site owned by the U.S. Air Force near Gakona, Alaska. There is only a 6 degree difference in latitude between HAARP in Alaska, and Skjervoy, Norway, where the Norway Spiral appeared. The LHC is located about 50 miles underground spanning the border of Geneva, Switzerland, and France. There are regular conspiracy theories about both locations. However, there are more eyebrows raised about HAARP because it conducts experiments directly on our atmosphere, which is already teetering from climate crisis and the 1970's dance with the Ozone layer, whereas the experiments in the LHC are contained in a big giant tube 50 miles underground.

Not to mention, the LHC is run by the European Organization for Nuclear Research – a group of tweed-wearing super nerds whose erotic fantasy is nuclear fusion– and HAARP is run by the Air Force (Air Force Research Laboratory), the Navy (Office of Naval Research and Naval Research Laboratory), and the Defense Advanced Research Projects Agency – all with oversight by the Department of Defense. So, as Bob from Sesame Street would say: One of these things is not like the other.

Just as early atomic tests were a shot in the dark, HAARP remains somewhat controversial to many because it deals in portions of our atmosphere about which we know little – the Ionosphere. Too high to reach with weather balloons and spy planes, and too low to reach with satellites, the Ionosphere is the atmospheric layer that we use in order to bounce radio and broadcast waves from Point A to Point B, across the globe. It's our radio ricochet point in the sky created by the Sun's powerful UV (Ultra Violet) energy. We know very little about what makes the Ionosphere tick because we have no way of testing its plasma – or the juice that gives our ricochet point its "bounce" -- short of shooting rockets into the Ionosphere and taking brief readings while they plummet.

We do know that when the northern lights are at their peak – or, when a solar flare burps millions of tons of radiation across the earth's magnetosphere – the Ionosphere then ignites like a pipeline, sending huge amounts of electromagnetic energy all over the world through its plasma network, like a round electric fence. Of course, this can negatively affect communication because our ricochet point is then full of signal-interrupting EMF (Electro Magnetic Fields). That's why cell phones and satellite-driven navigational equipment don't work well during solar flares. So in trying to understand the Ionosphere, we're trying to understand how to stabilize our communications network here on Earth. That's what they say on the HAARP website, anyway. As such, the scientists at HAARP range from world and government scientists to folks sent out by large communications companies. Oh yeah – and nearly all branches of the United States Military along with our national defense team. Yep, it's all just "science for the sake of science". Nothing to see here, people.

Since the military and science rarely go hand in hand without a strategic reason larger than a Verizon cell tower, let's discuss the white elephant in the room: If we understand the Ionosphere better, we understand the transference of Electromagnetic fields across the globe with greater accuracy – which means we then get a handle on not only what creates a Vortex, which is an enormous fold in the electromagnetic field, but where to find one. If we get a handle on the Earth's Vortex system, then just like our OffWorld friends, we, too, will be able to pop through wormholes from one quadrant of the galaxy to the other – or even just across the planet – in one step. The ET's that stepped through a "hatch" into my room after creating a "doorway" in my "basement floor", years ago, were taking advantage of the Electromagnetic properties of the natural ley lines beneath my childhood home to fold space through the naturally occurring Vortex point. The same Vortex in my bedroom also provided a doorway for countless other paranormal hitchhikers to cross from this dimension to the next. A freeway is a freeway. It doesn't matter what kind of car you drive; the road is the same.

From a military perspective, this Vortex system is the new railroad, the new airplane – and whoever decodes this "Stargate" information first – wins. As such, we aren't the only country working toward this decryption. In fact, one of the most well-known Vortex-related military actions was in 2009 at the Gulf of Aden. The naval might of twenty-seven countries was combined off the Somali coast to fight pirates who attacked the shipping lanes. At least, that's why they told all of us that this enormous worldwide armada had been amassed. Sure, there are pirates in the Gulf of Aden. Over 21,000 ships pass through the waterway each year, many with their tanker bellies full of oil as they leave the Red Sea and cross into the Indian Ocean. But a few Somali pirates raiding luxury yachts and an occasional mid-sized cargo tanker wouldn't demand the largest, most powerful naval force ever to be assembled in the history of humanity.

An expanding Vortex, however – would.

In late 2000, a magnetic Vortex was allegedly discovered in the Gulf of Aden by Admiral Maksimov of Russia's Northern Fleet. Russia, China and the United States jointly investigated the phenomenon and couldn't determine the cause. The Vortex was monitored and deemed as stable. In 2007, an earthquake registering the magnitude of 6.3 rattled the ocean floor in the Gulf of Aden. In 2008, the Vortex began to expand. This prompted the United States government to send an urgent call out to the world militaries, all of whom sent their warships -- unsure if the expansion of the Vortex meant an invasion.

We must remember that a door swings both ways. By understanding the earth's Vortex system, we may use wormholes not only for our own travel needs – but to anticipate someone else stepping through them. From a defensive standpoint, this would be helpful. Not that any earthly military could even begin to provide a lick of defense against any OffWorld attack, should they ever decide to put the smack down on Humanity. However, considering these races have been around far longer than we have, and don't really experience time like we do since they do so much temporal (time and space) travel, they could have easily "taken over the earth" long before we wrecked the oceans and the atmosphere. The real estate was a little more pristine before the industrial revolution, so clearly they aren't here to conquer us for our natural resources. That's a Human trait, to steal land, territory and customs.

No wonder we're paranoid.

So, because we're Human and paranoid, the HAARP antenna array is a major Arctic research facility (because nothing says Alien Vs Predator like an Arctic research facility) consisting of a really high-powered transmitter that operates in the High Frequency range. This is an important part of our geek puzzle because High Frequencies excite particles – or make them move around really fast – and when they move around, you can observe a lot more about them. The downside of high frequency particle excitement is that if you get those particles moving too quickly, they bust apart other particles that are unfortunately just hanging around, like an indiscriminant drunk guy swinging wide in a bar fight. Thus, the effectiveness of Ultra-Sonic washing machines, Ultra-Sonic toothbrushes, and so on. You get the drift. Now, we're not pumping ultra-sonic waves into the atmosphere. At least they tell us we're not. But there are a whole lot of folks who have a vision of the

HAARP Array blowing apart our atmosphere in our attempt to open up wormholes. Um, I mean – in our study of the Ionosphere.

And maybe they aren't all wearing tin foil hats, considering the HAARP transmitter delivers up to 3.6 million watts to the antenna array, beaming 3.6 million watts of pure high-frequency excitement into the atmosphere. To put this into perspective, one of those big, tall commercial FM radio towers, the same one that ruins your view, eats up 150,000 watts of electricity to cover a radius of 40 miles. As you can see, HAARP is pumping a lot of juice. But in fairness, it's not just pumping to one antennae – it's pumping electricity to 180 antennae across 33 acres, arranged as a great big rectangular grid called a Planar Array. All the antennae work as one gigantic ray gun, shooting high sound frequencies into the "flesh" of the Ionosphere, hitting an overhead patch of atmosphere about 20 to 30 miles in diameter and a few hundred yards thick. HAARP then listens for the slap-back, or echo, off this patch, and analyzes the data to figure out what's going on up there, like super-powered sonar.

Won't this hurt the atmosphere like the tin foil hat tribe says that it will, you ask?

Well, again, in fairness to science rather than hysteria, considering that the Ionosphere is way, way up in the sky, our gigantic High Frequency mega beam loses a lot of its oomph once it hits the Ionosphere, amounting to an impact that is thousands of times less than the Sun's natural electromagnetic radiation reaching the earth, and even hundreds of times less than the Sun's natural ultraviolet (UV) energy which creates the Ionosphere in the first place. So we really are the mosquito on the back of the horse here.

That being said, there are people who swear that due to the fact that we know so little about how the Ionosphere works, the introduction of super-high frequencies into the plasma will have unforeseen results. In fact, it could, yet welcome to American science. When we exploded the first atomic test bomb in the New Mexico desert on July 16th, 1945, at 5:29 a.m., we weren't even sure that the blast could be contained to splitting *only* the atoms in the bomb. Heck, as far as we knew, it could have set off a chain reaction that split every atom on the earth, like a never-ending trail of toppling dominos, blowing apart the whole planet on a molecular level in an instant.

But hey, we weren't going to know unless we tried, right?

And, though we may only be nicking the surface of the Ionosphere itself with the HAARP Array, we're not the only country doing it. So there's no telling how introducing this intense high-frequency beam is going to affect other layers in our overall atmosphere while on its way up. Sheesh, as it stands, HAARP has to issue a warning to the FAA to re-route flights in the area once testing has commenced, lest an unsuspecting airliner pass through such a high emission of EMF from the transmitter and lose all power.

Between the use of Vortexes for travel and the bending of space, our OffWorld cousins seem to have quite a handle on our world in a way we simply don't. There is a lot about OffWorlders that we don't understand.

At least that much -- we do know.

*Part iii - Hijacked and LoJacked*

Over the years, I attempted to get a handle on what had occurred in my bedroom in 1991. By 1993, I had left Montana and had been living in Seattle for a few years. I had started into the music industry and had my first record deal with an independent label in the Emerald City. I was living with my partner at the time and her mother in a renovated old historic home off of Martin Luther King Jr. Way. This wasn't the best area of town, but it wasn't the worst. It was definitely an urban area, heavily populated.

After my experience in my Montana bedroom years before, I preferred to sleep against a wall. I learned that the guy on the outside of the bed has a better chance of being rolled off the bed into a glowing hole in the floor by ET's, so I'd take my chances scrunched up against the sheetrock.

I experienced disturbing dreams in the house, although overall, the house really had a warm vibe. Many of the dreams had to do with cupboards being open by themselves, or my dresser drawers all strewn open one way or the other while the lights would not turn on. The feeling in the dreams was that someone that I could not see was in the house. This was not entirely shocking, as the house was also haunted. I dismissed the dreams as the ghosts in the home reaching out in my twilight time. I was far too busy being a rock star to worry about any phantoms in a rental home.

One night, my partner and I turned in rather early. She was dead asleep, and I was doing what I always did, which was to lay in bed for a good half hour before sleep would claim me. I had my back to my partner and I was facing the wall. It was a nice little cubbyhole in which to wind down.

On the wall not a foot from my face appeared a rippling yellow light. It danced up the wall in a small square no more than 18 inches, feathery, like a glowing boa, reflections from a golden pool somewhere else. The hypnotic yellow lights were back.

I wasn't falling for it twice. I immediately began to think, "Oh, no, I'm not --!" when my conscious thought was interrupted.

I was suddenly plunged into a dream. I looked around, wondering how I got there so quickly from my bedroom, and I was sitting on the floor in a circle with maybe fifteen other people. In the center of the circle was a forest green ten gallon trash can – the Rubbermaid kind that are in everyone's kitchen. I realized that this was some sort of classroom. The woman leading the class looked like a typical metaphysical woman in her early 50's, with the shoulder length natural tight curl hair and the flowing gauze skirts and beads. She spoke in an extremely calming tone of voice.

"I want all of you to take hands, and focus on the trash can in the center of the circle. Using the power of your mind, I want us to raise the trash can together," she said.

We all took hands, and focused. But this felt so strange. The entire time, I was a touch bewildered, and thinking: "How did I get to sleep so quickly?"

The trash can warbled and raised an inch, but then set back down. I got up from the circle and headed for the doorway. I wasn't sure how I ended up in this dream, or how I fell asleep so quickly, but I wasn't too hip on playing "light as a feather" with a garbage can, some hippie chick, and a bunch of people I didn't know. I figured if this was a dream, I'd head for some more interesting pastures.

I walked out of the doorway – and right back into the room. The woman who was instructing addressed me in that warm, lulling tone of voice. "Please, have a seat. We need everyone involved if we're going to raise the trash can."

I stood there for a moment, and I noticed that everyone else in the circle was either looking at the trash can, or had their head bowed and their eyes closed. This instructor was the only one who was engaging me. She was seated and she patted the floor next to her for me to sit. I wasn't sure I wanted to do that, but it was a dream – or whatever it was – and I didn't have anywhere else to go. So, I walked around the circle and sat down.

"We must all hold hands to focus the energy," she said, taking my hand.

Again, we all focused on the trash can. It began to rise off the floor, levitating.

"Good," she said. "That's very good. Continue to focus."

As we were all looking at this trash can, I noticed that the instructor to my left looked different in my periphery than she did when I looked directly at her. When viewing her head on, she was the classic 1970's granola-eating earth goddess. Yet in my periphery, she was much more trim – lanky, even. Her body was much longer, and so was her neck. In fact, her arms were much longer and skinnier than they should have been. As I was making note of this, the trash can started to wobble and sink.

The instructor chimed in again, a touch more firm in her approach, but still incredibly calm. "Please, we need everyone to focus on the trash can."

I turned my attention back to the Rubbermaid in the center of the circle, and it began to rise again. For a circle of maybe fifteen strangers, we were doing pretty well – that trash can was floating about three feet up in the air. I couldn't help but notice that her hand seemed cold in mine. I remember wanting to look down at her hand. Then a feeling came through her hand and up my arm, a definite feeling of imploring me to simply focus on the task. It wasn't a threatening feeling. In fact, it was more of a desperate feeling. She wasn't speaking, but I could hear her, in my head. It wasn't a voice, but a message transmitted to me under the fabric of this dreamscape:

"Please. We've gone through all this trouble to create this for you, so you won't be afraid."

It was a very honest feeling. And, this woman genuinely seemed to be on my side. In fact, it seemed as though this entire thing had been her idea. The underbelly of her comment had components that I was uncomfortable picking up – the inference that if I chose to snap out of whatever dreamscape this was – the alternative would be far more terrifying.

I knew she was sincere. And I wasn't up for terrifying. Plus, I didn't want to let her down. For some reason, I felt as if this woman was the singular advocate for me being treated to this "dream", rather than whatever was the alternative.

Quite suddenly, I was acutely aware that this was some form of distraction. I looked down at her hand, in mine – which consisted of two thick finger stalks and a thumb, the color of chalk. Though there was compassion coming through the hand – the hand was not Human.

I didn't have time to react to what I saw, as I was plunged further into another dream that I can barely remember. Something about being outside in the sun, in a crowd of people at a country fair, and music was playing. I remember feeling lost, and irritated at how fuzzy the dream was, and trying to run back to find the building that the garbage can brigade had taken residence in, so I could find a doorway out, then BAM – I was slammed farther into another dream. This time, the dream was so daunting that it had my full attention. I lost myself in the act of the nightmare, hiding from Nazis in the dark, as search lights and barking dogs combed the scrub brush in which I hid – the sound of bombs exploding in the darkness, and people screaming orders in German.

I popped awake, and the sun was shining. My partner had gone to work, and I was alone in the house. It was a crisp October day and the house felt peaceful, though I was at a loss as to how I had gone from such a disturbing dream right into such a peaceful morning. I realized immediately what had occurred.

Seeing as that years prior, the Ethereal Elephant Dart didn't work very well, my ET friends had figured out a method of anesthesia that would work on me. They knocked me out completely into a dream state, rather than trying the "half conscious" physical approach. Lord only knows to where I was actually hauled off, or what they were doing. I doubt they had a Rubbermaid endorsement. I was in the middle of Seattle, but with their ability to bend space, I don't think the neighbors were disturbed.

I realized once awake that the "woman" in the dream, the instructor, wasn't a woman at all. I remembered her eyes – they were too large. And her hand with three fingers – well, two fingers and a thumb, with a rather scaly appearance – wasn't a very convincing Human mock-up. But, in some universal dimension somewhere, she had been holding my hand, in real time, and I knew it. This ET really, sincerely didn't want me to be afraid. She had a distinct singular consciousness, rather than the group consciousness of the beings that had entered my bedroom in Montana. This woman, or female, though not as emotional as a Human being, had a deep maternal compassion. And she seemed to be concerned for my state of mind.

Either that or these entities knew I'd respond to that approach, and she, too, was nothing more than an effective illusion concocted to keep me distracted in feeling safe. In retrospect however, I would truly vouch for the fact that this entity was indeed a real being, cast into an unreal environment to keep me focused. Living creatures have a very specific resonance.

When I wouldn't stay focused on the dream, given positive distractions, my dream was turned to a nightmare. I don't think this was her choice. The Nazi dream had an entirely different feel. I kept trying to crawl out of the positive dream and back into what was really happening, back to my bed in Seattle. It's a touch sad that I could not be distracted by positive influence. When the nightmare was turned on, I lost my awareness that it was all a dream, and started participating with the frightening storyline. Yet in hindsight, I don't think I gave them much choice. For whatever reason, it was very important to them that I "stay under".

I encountered ETs the entire duration of living in Seattle, though the incident in the renovated house was the last of the dancing yellow light abductions. Well, that I'm aware of, anyway. Seattle seemed to be crawling with these peach-colored "gray" type OffWorlders. This comes as no surprise when one realizes that only 44 miles away is Joint Base Lewis-McChord, a super-military compound that combines Fort Lewis Army Base and McChord Air Force Base. Housing around 19,000 people, JBLM is the 6th largest military base in the country. Where you find the military, you find Grays.

For instance, in 1992, I was living in an apartment located on Capitol Hill, another very populated part of Seattle. A group of us had been out on the back patio enjoying the night view of the Seattle skyline when a bizarre glowing blue rectangle appeared on the roof of the home next door. It was maybe six inches wide by about five feet long. It scanned the roof, stopping, tracking back, then continued forward. It had a decidedly mechanical movement as it slowly combed the roof, like an automated barcode scanner. It was creepy. No one in the group could locate the source from which this blue light was being projected, and everyone was unnerved. Considering this was a group of very liberal political activists in our fearless early 20's, the caution we all felt was noted. I found myself being the one who insisted we go inside before it reached us on the patio. I knew what this thing was, scanning the home next door for the life forms inside. Don't ask me how I knew this, but I did.

We all went inside and I locked the door (because flipping a rusty deadbolt in defense against a species that manipulates space-time is surely to be effective, right?). The group filtered off into the apartment and I stayed in the living room. I could feel something outside the apartment, over the block – I didn't have quite the command of my sixth sense abilities back then, but even then I knew I was very sensitive to energy fields. Something was in the house, and it wasn't the resonance of a human spirit.

I stayed behind in the living room without telling anyone what I was sensing as it really did all seem a little too Woo-woo back then, even for a group of anti-war activists. I was looking out the large picture window over the city, waiting. In the reflection of the window, I saw this little peach-colored figure, three feet tall, bulbous head, small body with a little pot belly – reflected from inside the apartment. This little dude was standing in the dining room behind me. Just as my eyes focused on him (he felt male), he realized I saw him in the reflection, and he side-stepped behind the kitchen wall.

I bolted for the kitchen behind me, not two seconds away. I rounded the corner – and I could see nothing but an empty kitchen. But I could feel him. He was a few feet from me, to the right, standing quietly, as if he'd accidently stepped on a twig in the woods and drawn attention to himself. I could feel his stillness, like a mouse freezing in the open while a predator circled, hoping to blend into the brush. He felt very young.

My telepathic connection with these beings was kicked wide open and I was flooded with information about this little guy: They had placed him in the house as a test exercise to get him accustomed to being around Humans. He was there to observe, and to overcome his fear of our species. I'm assuming he would be later assigned to some 24-hour Abduction Crew, and maybe this was how they got their youth over their fear of us giant, violent, knuckle-dragging Homo sapiens -- sort of like how divers submerge in the South African waters to swim with Great White Sharks.

Anyway, for as much as these beings have any sort of emotionality, he felt "scared". Not scared like we'd be scared, but very aware of the fact that he'd done something wrong. He was not afraid of me, but of the consequences of his mistake once he returned to the beings that sent him here. I felt sorry for him. I've come to learn that the Grays are a rather heartless ET species, mostly with their own, only because they lack the spiritual components that create our complex understanding of cause and effect.

Thanks to this telepathic connection, I understood what he'd done incorrectly. The dimensional cloaking device used by this OffWorld species, and many others, actually, involves "bending light". Well, not actually bending the LIGHT itself, but bending the space around which the light reflects. Think of wrapping yourself up in the drapes, when you were a kid. If your parents couldn't see your feet, you were invisible in the room. These OffWorlders are able to "wrinkle" space-time, step into the wrinkle, and then allow light to bounce off the surface of the wrinkle. Thanks to my handy-dandy telepathic trivia dump, I realized that stepping into the wrinkle is only effective if you're looking right at the wrinkle. A reflection is light bounced at an angle. Thus, this poor little guy could easily be seen standing in the dining room, when viewed in the reflection.

Busted.

Again, thanks to my telepathic ticker-tape, I could "hear" his senior trainers telepathically conversing with him about his misstep. It appears they knew he'd fumble in this regard. They were giving him a hard time, but I could tell that the "hard time" was more a show. They expected him to blow it. Apparently, this is one of the first mistakes that young OffWorlders make when using this technology. Sort of like how young law enforcement officers forget to take the safety off of the gun in the heat of the moment.

Had I been thinking on my feet, I would've grabbed some sort of pan or reflective surface in the kitchen, and glanced into it to get another look at the little guy. But I was more fixated on feeling sorry for him, and honestly, I knew where he was standing. I could feel him.

"I know you're here," I said quietly, as not to alert my pals in the other room that I was talking to an invisible Alien. "And I'd like you to leave, please."

Considering the exercise was a wash on his part, the being turned on his heel and zipped right through the outside wall. The static feeling in the apartment subsided, and the space immediately felt better.

The second time I encountered OffWorlders of this ilk was in 1994, in Steilacoom, WA, which is only around ten miles from Joint Base Lewis-McChord. At the time, I was with my partner "Keira" at my aunt's home. We were staying in her daylight basement while transitioning to move back to Montana. I had been signed to a small Northwest record label, and upon fulfilling the contract, I was done. One album and three vinyl singles later, I was cut loose, having not "hit" like the other Northwest goldmines known later as Nirvana and Pearl Jam. Like most kids in their early 20's, I ran through my money, spending what little rock star funds I'd accrued on important things like cool guitars rather than Starbucks stock options (which I was offered and didn't take because I was a young employee with the money sense of a single-celled organism). Broke, without a record deal, and no longer wishing to bug my well-intentioned dad with my financial issues – he'd been bailing me out -- it was time to head back to my home state. Keira was heading with me.

The rest of the family was out for the night. We were watching TV in the basement when we both had this uncanny feeling of being watched through the open windows. Of course, it was nighttime, so the pitch black of the evening was the only thing peering through the panes. However, the feeling was ominous enough that we both wanted the curtains closed. There was a static feeling in the ethers – the type of sterile EMF field that crackles in the air and accompanies OffWorlders and their technology.

Keira wasn't one for buying into the idea of ghosts, or Aliens, or anything that wasn't of this world, really. Yet even Keira was unnerved, her own extrasensory abilities being tapped by the overwhelming pressure of the EMF.

To add to the eeriness, the empty house upstairs was suddenly filled with the sound of many little feet scurrying across the floorboards. I looked at Keira and she looked at me, and we ended up hunched behind the closed door that led out of the basement upstairs. On the other side of the door was part of the split level home's staircase that led to the landing and the front door. Then, turning on a dime, one could head all the way upstairs up the second staircase.

Keira was as wigged as I was at this point. The fact that she was wigged didn't make me feel any better, as Keira wasn't the "scared" type. I looked around the basement and found a baseball bat. Now, deep down, both of us knew that whatever lay upstairs would not likely be phased by a baseball bat. However, the fact that I had the bat made me feel a whole lot better, and when we're talking unknowns, sometimes a Louisville Slugger goes a long way.

The basement door was locked. I looked at Keira, and she looked at me, and we had a quick discussion about whether or not it was a good idea to head upstairs. I decided that it was better to face whatever was up there head on, rather than waiting like weird trapped mice in the basement. Clearly, if something was deft enough to get into the house without alerting us, then they knew we were here in the first place. Prior to the scuttle upstairs, the daylight basement curtains had been wide open and we were rather visible from outside while watching TV.

I unlocked basement the door. The scurrying continued upstairs. There had to be at least six or seven of whatever these were, by the sound of the quick little feet darting about. I grabbed the Louisville Slugger a little tighter, and slowly opened the door.

The scurrying upstairs stopped abruptly.

I stopped abruptly.

Keira was huddled behind me. Nearly holding my breath in the sudden silence, I continued to slowly open the basement door. The short split staircase lay in front of me. I had a clear view of the landing, but because of the architecture of these 1980's split level homes, I couldn't see upstairs – only the sheetrock wall. My heart was racing. It was too quiet.

I took one step up, then another, so very quietly and so carefully, all the while listening upstairs for any movement. There was nothing. Keira followed closely behind me. I could feel her holding onto the back of my shirt. And I could feel several entities upstairs, standing dead still.

I took one more step, then another – this wasn't a very long portion of the staircase. I was only a few steps from reaching the landing and I could see the door very clearly. The door had this oversized but beautiful polished brass knob in the inside. And staring at me in the reflection of the handle – upside down, of course, because of the curvature of the door knob – was a perfect reflection of a stereotypical Extra Terrestrial, with the huge almond shaped eyes, tiny mouth, tiny nostrils, and bulbous head.

I froze. I couldn't believe what I was looking at. I was standing two steps below the landing, and it had to be standing two steps above the landing, around the corner on the other split staircase. This thing was right through the sheetrock wall, to my left – right next to me. We were both frozen; seeing what the other would do. My deepest fears were confirmed.

The house was swarming with Grays.

"Are you seeing that?" I said to Keira under my breath.

"Yes," she answered. I didn't even need to describe what I was seeing. The reflection was incredibly obvious.

"What does that look like to you?" I half whispered.

"Come on, come on --" she said as she frantically yanked me by the shirt backwards, and down the stairs to the safety of the basement.

We locked the door – again, because surely, one of those in-handle twisty-locks would be able to keep out a species that somehow beamed into the home from some other universe. But it's all we had at the moment. Well, that and the baseball bat, and both options seemed pretty piddly at that point.

"You saw that, right?" I blurted quietly, wanting to double confirm in the moment that the disbelieving Keira had witnessed the same thing that I did.

"That's a [swear word] Alien," she answered, eyes wide -- as matter-of-fact as can be.

Yep. Grays. She heard them, and I heard them. She saw them, and I saw them. And we both felt completely screwed, standing behind a locked door in the basement.

As such, we both kicked into instinctual hyper-drive, running around the basement and shutting off the lights and the TV, crouching in the dark by a corner of the sofa where we had a good strategic view of the basement door, the sliding door that lead to outside, and all the windows.

The Human survival instinct is intense, and unless one is ever in a situation where logic can no longer be applied and pure adrenalized animal instinct kicks in, one can never fully appreciate the fact that in reality, we are only a few chromosomes shy from being wild beasts. As a modernized society, we pride ourselves on our logic, our reason, and our rational problem solving. We take comfort in our guns, our traps, and our poisons, and in this comfort, we see ourselves as the top of the food chain, forgetting that it's our gadgets -- and not us – that keep us there. In our hubris, and what I believe is our internalized Mammal-Phobia, we have wholeheartedly disassociated from our biological animal nature as a result of no longer having to fend for our existence in the wild. We claim to be controlled conscious heads on top of suits, controlled conscious heads in jars at work, and all the while, a raging pornography industry thrives in cubicles across America. In shameful secret, we reduce our intrinsic mammalian instincts to a debased industry where reproduction has been made into entertainment – all to justify our need to connect on a level that has no rationale, no logic, and no reason. In our utter fear that we are animals – we have become animals. Yet we always were, with DNA that is a 98.5% match to that of a chimpanzee.

Let me tell you – that chimpanzee part comes in handy in a crisis. As a species, when we are physically threatened, there are a host of tricks and tips that flood into play that we never knew we even had in our survival arsenal. I have a fight instinct, not a flight instinct. But when I saw the reflection of that other-wordly thing in the doorknob, even I assessed that I wasn't going to win that one with sheer Montana grit and a Louisville Slugger. Something kicked in that said "Big predator -- hide." Like rabbits taking cover under a clump of grass while evading a prowling mountain lion – Keira and I hoped for the best.

As we grew quiet in the dark, the scurrying upstairs resumed. The movement was hesitant this time, as if the entire gang up there was attempting to tip-toe. The staircase creaked as something walked up the stairs and away from the landing, confirming that our X-Files buddy had indeed been parked right around the corner on the staircase right next to me.

Slowly, the sounds of movement upstairs trailed off. There was no dramatic exit, just…eventually, nothing. They silently evaporated back into wherever it was they silently came from. Again – this species is fairly on top of the whole space-bending thing. We waited for quite some time in the dark silence of the basement until we turned on the light. When we went upstairs, all the kitchen cupboard doors were left wide open, including the drawers.

Keira stared. So did I. I remember being equal parts freaked out and struck with the curious notion that perhaps this entire terrifying time our OffWorld Friends had simply run out of Ragu. Let's face it – I don't care what quadrant of the galaxy that you're from – running out of eats in the middle of a dinner party is just bad form.

As it turns out, one of the down-to-earth residents of this house, "Carl", repeatedly spoke about "dreams" involving little hooded men in the front yard, bright frightening lights, floating craft, and the utter phobia of Alien abduction. It's a wonderful mercy our subconscious provides by protecting us from the horrifying truth.

A few days later, Keira and I moved to back to Montana. And none too soon.

I looked back on the incident at a later time and realized that I was able to see the ET because it was reflected in the doorknob. I'm 100% positive that had I mustered the nerve to round the corner and look up the stairs – I would have seen nothing. This species can bend light with the finesse of Madonna's same-sex kisses in front of the paparazzi. Though no one is as good as Madonna – these ET's are very good at what they do. And, it's likely that the Vortex point of exit from the home was in the kitchen, causing the cupboard doors and drawers to swing open toward the center of the room where the pull of gravity would intensify as the wormhole opened.

Ironically, one year earlier, early in 1993, I visited my first Psychic in Seattle -- who removed what she called an "Alien implant" from my crown chakra. I went to see her on a lark because I was having problems praying. Well, I wasn't having problems praying, but I felt like something was cutting me off, from the top of my head up. It was more like I felt as though my prayers were being snatched away on their way up to God – it was hard to explain. My only metaphysical friend at the time, "Judy", told me that, perhaps maybe, it was a spiritual issue, and referred me to a Psychic -- a broom handle of a woman with a bad perm who had mugged Stevie Nicks for her clothes.

I was a Christian kid from Montana. I thought this Psychic was a Pagan nut job.

But there I was, trying to be respectful, because occultist wacko or not, Judy had paid for the appointment with this Psychic and I was raised to be polite. I didn't even know what a chakra was. When she told me it was akin to an energy field, I couldn't understand how some sort of implant would exist in some pretend energy field – and then I really thought she was a nut job. I was pretty sure her Lorraine Newman perm had seeped through her scalp and had eaten her brain. She went on to explain that I had some sort of "energetic net" implanted in my crown chakra (…nut job…) whose purpose was to monitor my spiritual communication with God (…come again?…). When I asked her how it got there, she explained to me that there was a race of ET's --- Grays -- who were void of spiritual expression, yet they yearned for it, and they were highly curious as to our ability to connect to a higher source – or God. Basically, in a nutshell, this race lacked the spiritual Bluetooth technology that humans possess. I had not yet told her of my ongoing saga with OffWorlders, and I knew that Judy hadn't either.

I retracted my ruling of "nut job", stopped being so judgmental, and decided to listen.

I asked her why I would end up having one of these net-thingies in my crown shock-a-whatever, and she told me that I must have some sort of spiritual ability that they were interested in. I didn't understand what she meant by "spiritual ability". I asked her what ability, and she became a touch testy and said she didn't know, but it must be something important if they were trying to monitor my communications with "Source". She told me that an implant of this nature was very unusual, quite large covering my whole head, and that she had never seen something as complicated. She described a type of energetic webbing. She told me it was "deeply imbedded" in my crown chakra because it had been in there a very long time -- since I was very young -- and it had something to do with family lineage. Then she asked me if I wanted it removed.

Well, duh – yes, please remove the multi-generational prayer-blocking Alien implant, Stevie Nicks.

The Psychic was sitting on one couch, and I was on another. I asked her what I should do during this implant removal process, and she told me to sit quietly. Easy enough. She closed her eyes and placed her hands on her knees. I sat there feeling awkward in the silence, looking at her. And that's when it happened.

I felt an enormous physical pressure from the back of my head. I felt as though someone was trying to pry the top of my skull off. It didn't hurt but the pressure was uncomfortable. This wasn't all just psychological – my entire body began to rise off the couch cushions, as if someone was attempting to pry a tight helmet off my head, and it just wasn't giving. The more they pulled, the more I was raised up off the cushions, like a dangling marionette. I heard the leather cushions shift beneath me. I was genuinely shocked that whatever she was doing over there, without touching me, was having an actual physical effect on me across the room. Just as this was starting to get very uncomfortable, the invisible helmet gave -- and popped off. I felt the SNAP, I dropped back into the couch, and I very clearly heard and saw this burst of beautifully tweeting birds – swallows or sparrows – singing and flying into the distance, as if the flock had been trapped beneath this net for a very long time.

It was not a hallucination. The flock of birds whisked past me and out the window – though the glass window pane was closed. I said nothing. What could I say? This was all way out of my wheelhouse at the time. The Psychic immediately opened her eyes.

"There," she stated. "It's gone."

How would she have known that? She had her eyes closed – she couldn't have seen me rising up off the couch as this implant was being pulled from my energy field. Maybe she heard the birds? Good God, if that's the case, then that would just confirm the birds were indeed -- real.

She went on to tell me many more fascinating things that have all come to pass. And I've never had personal problems with OffWorlders since.

*Part iv - Gray Genes in Blue Jeans*

You can take the girl out of the space ship, but you just can't take the space ship out of the girl. Or maybe it can be done, but due to the nature of my Empathic and Psychic connections to pretty much all energy around me, I get the extreme pleasure of remaining connected to the ET Network even though they have no idea I'm a subscriber.

Huh. Free cable. Well, that's a different perspective…

The fact is, due to the ~~irritating~~ fascinating way in which I'm wired -- to catalogue any and all energetic imprints with which I come into contact -- I still pick up the frequencies of all Gray communications. I'm a ham radio that has never been turned off.

How glamorous.

But I know I'm not on their abduction radar anymore. They can't find me. The Grays so lack the ability to tell us apart from within that without a third-party LoJack, they don't know how to tell the difference in the make or model of the car they're trying to steal. It's really quite tragic – they seek to study our spiritual make-up, yet can't identify us by our spirit. In fact, they tend to follow logs that chronicle family lines which exhibit spiritual abilities. The implants are somewhat of a crapshoot. They may net something, or they may not, depending on the sea turtle they tag.

This species is so different from us, so uniform in how they are designed, that our individuality goes widely unnoticed by them. They fixate on our likenesses. It's how they are able to relate to us. The Grays are not evil, nor maniacal. They don't have enough emotionality for maniacal, though they are very singular-minded in executing their agenda, and to we emotional human beings – that could seem tyrannical

114

and heartless. They simply don't share anything at all in common with us – spiritually, culturally, or physically – except that the same Parent Creator God made us both. Plus, they seem to have an issue with their own genetics, and reproduction, for whatever reason. The closest thing I can uncover on their genetic front is that they reproduce externally, not having any reproductive organs as we would recognize them. They also tend to endlessly tinker with their own genome. So over time, while trying to make the "perfect" Gray (because this species is INSANE when it comes to efficiency), they've sort of tweaked-out their own genetics by augmenting too much information. Just as we genetically adjust produce here on earth, the Grays have augmented themselves. In order for us to genetically adjust a tomato so that it won't rot as quickly, the removal of the "rot" gene (to paraphrase) also removes the gene that controls some of the tomato's flavor. Once the new, genetically modified tomato produces seeds, the former flavor of the non-genetically altered tomato becomes a thing of the past, as it's no longer included in the DNA of the new seed. To gain something, we lose something. This seems to also be the case with the Grays.

They're not only a tad obsessed with our Bluetooth ability to connect to God, but with our body's ability to regenerate and fix itself. This is one reason they end up snagging eggs from the female of our species, and cow parts including their many stomachs. The Grays don't pass waste through a big long slinky tube called intestines. Any waste they would accrue from the weird way that they "eat" comes out through the pores of their skin. They "eat" differently, too – a pasty liquid stuff that feels like sea plankton but God only knows what it is – so it's not like they're trying to push a pizza through their pores. Their bodies are interesting because they are mostly biological, with a synthetic additive that has been assimilated into their biology on a molecular level. Again, I can only attribute this introduction to their endless DNA tinkering. This synthetic material behaves like components in bone, and helps secure their skeletal structure.

Here on earth, we actually have in our possession a skull from one of our Gray pals. The skull is labeled as "The Star Child Skull", and, well, looks like the skull of a Gray. Found by a young girl in a cave southwest of Chihuahua, Mexico, back in 1930, the skull is estimated by archeologists to be 900 years old. People theorize that it's a human-Alien hybrid due to the fact that it was found entwined in the arms of a human female. To me, it looks all Gray, right down to the description of a "misshapen hand" that was originally reaching up through dirt floor of the cave – alerting the young girl to the skeletal presence below. The young girl took as souvenirs the skull from the human "mother" as well as took the other weird skull. In the 1990's, the woman died, and the skulls went to another man, who figured the Star Child Skull was that of a deformed baby. He then passed on the skulls to a neonatal nurse and her husband. Obviously, the nurse was familiar with human deformities, and was struck with the fact that this unusual skull did not fit the "deformed" format. It was extremely symmetrical in its proportions; much more so than would be a human skull, and was much too lightweight. The nurse also found it odd that the skull's eye sockets contained holes which would place the optic nerve in the wrong spot for a human. Not to mention the eye sockets were much too shallow.

The nurse had the skull examined. In 2003, credentialed experts in the USA, the UK, and Canada partook in detailed research, including microscopic analysis of multiple bone preparations, bone composition analysis, X-ray analysis, CT scan analysis, radiocarbon dating (C-14), cranial analysis, scanning electron microscopy (SEM), statistical analysis, inorganic chemistry analysis, and dental analysis. Further investigation of the skull resulted in the ruling out of any cosmetic skull deformation that would result from tribal practices of the day, such as skull binding. The super-team even debunked naturally occurring explanations for the overall shape of the skull, ruling out genetic and birth defects. For the final touch, extensive DNA testing was executed on the Star Child Skull by Trace Genetics of Davis, California. Trace Genetics has since been acquired by DNA Print Genomics in 2005. But at the time, its two owners and lead geneticists were Dr. Ripan Malhi and Dr. Jason Eshleman, both noted as specialists in their field, particularly in the area of recovering and identifying ancient DNA. Considering that science guys don't really want to be known as "the Alien-whisperer" around the water cooler – that tends to have a really discrediting effect later on down the road – these fellows were darn sure of what they were releasing into the world. The test results concluded that The Star Child Skull was not entirely human.

Scientifically – the skull was just weird.

A further 2011 Genetics Test on the Star Child skull revealed that there were not just a few, but 17 key differences between the Star Child's genome and human DNA. It turns out that the 2003 testing, though thorough, was only executed on a small portion of the skull's DNA, searching specifically for anything that would match human DNA. In effect, the search parameters for the sample ended up being too small. The 2011 test was more comprehensive, and logged far more differences in the skull's DNA. Considering that only a few differences are necessary to establish a new species, with a whopping 17 catalogued, the Star Child is, by scientific definition, a new species never before recorded on earth.

The 2003 tests indicated that a few DNA markers in the Star Child Skull matched the human sequence in the mitochondrial DNA, or the DNA passed on only from the mother. However, after six failed attempts at locating the Nuclear DNA, or the DNA that contains information from both parents, the scientists had to throw in the towel, as the Nuclear DNA information was so foreign it could not be identified. This started rumors that the Star Child was a human-Alien hybrid, with a human mom and an Alien dad. However, further genetic testing in 2011 exposed the fact that the very genetic markers scientists once labeled as "definitely human" actually came back as "human-like", so the skull could belong to something that was never human, but shared human traits. Add to this fascinating mystery the fact that the skull itself is much stronger than human bone, much thinner, and as viewed under en electron microscope, is comprised of not only what we'd recognize as traditional bone material, but a never-before-seen synthetic fiber that's bonded to the organic material in a way that we can't comprehend – and we have ourselves the skull of a bona fide Gray.

If it were 1860, that freaky-looking skull would have made a trek nationwide from carnival to carnival, viewed for a penny right before the bearded lady and right after the fire-breather. But we live in much more banal times, so we'll have to settle for a genetic report rather than a hand-painted banner heralding the nail-biting arrival of the "Monster Cave Boy".

Though I'm no big fan of the Grays, I believe every race has an upside, monster or not. The strength of this race is in their unity. They work as one. The downside is that they are a hive mind, so mob rules, and there is no such thing as a case-by-case review of any situation. I realized how magnificent Humanity is by viewing us through their eyes: They are puzzled and fascinated by our ability to be a rolling, boiling pot of chaos that manages to correspond our lives across the globe, live out a lifespan, have children, have faith, all independent from one another, then eject ourselves out of this flesh suit and back into the heart of God from which we came -- all on instinct. They have no idea how this is able to occur without a blatant telepathic connection, like they possess. War of the Worlds would never work out in the Alien's favor if it were the Grays that were levying the attack as they just simply have no idea how to anticipate us.

I'm not certain if it was my time acting as a traveling implant docking station, or if it's a side-effect of my Clairaudience and Psychic abilities, but I'm still very tied to the Grays. The Grays are hive mind, and much like Picard on Star Trek, once assimilated as part of the Borg, you always hear the Borg, even if you escape the Borg. Though unlike the Borg – resistance is not futile when dealing with the Grays. As a former tagged sea turtle, I know what they're up to, I know when they're around, I know how their technology works, and I know how long they've been contracted to work with our military. We're not the first military they've worked with, pairing up first with Nazi Germany. That should illustrate the conscienceless nature of these entities.

One doesn't have to be Psychic to be familiar with these ET's. Henry H. McElroy, a former Republican in the New Hampshire House of Representative, released a video in 2010 regarding his eye-witness account of a briefing given to President Eisenhower in regard to meeting with Extra Terrestrials. The following is a portion of Rep. McElroy's speech as transcribed from his video, posted on YouTube.

*March 11, 2010*

*"I would like to submit to our nation my personal testimony of one document related to one of these ongoing topics which I saw while in office, serving on the State Federal Relations and Veterans Affairs Committee.*

*The document I saw was an official brief to President Eisenhower. To the best of my memory this brief was pervaded with a sense of hope, and it informed President Eisenhower of the continued presence of extraterrestrial beings here in the United States of America.*

*The brief seemed to indicate that a meeting between the President and some of these visitors could be arranged as appropriate if desired.*

*The tone of the brief indicated to me that there was no need for concern, since these visitors were in no way causing any harm, or had any intentions, whatsoever, of causing any disruption then, or in the future."*

This account by Rep. McElroy resonates with two accounts of Eisenhower meeting with ETs, back in 1954. The meetings were said to have taken place at Holloman Air Force Base in New Mexico, and Muric-Edwards Air Force Base in California. Supposedly, Eisenhower first met with a benevolent ET race which not only looks very similar to human beings, but walks among us here. They warned the President of dealing with Grays, describing the species as ruthless, self-serving, and untrustworthy. That tale seems to match up with Rep. McElroy's account – at least, the part about meeting with benevolent ETs.

The rest of the story is supported by accounts from Philip Schneider, former Captain in the United States Navy. Captain Schneider was part of Operation Crossroads, which tested nuclear weapons at Bikini Island in the Pacific. He went on to be a government structural engineer and was involved in the construction of underground military bases throughout the United States. Captain Schneider claimed to be one of only three people out of 63 to have survived the 1979 underground showdown between Grays and the Military that occurred in a cavern. Captain Schneider confirmed that in 1954, President Eisenhower signed the Greada Treaty with the Grays – who promised to give the United States technological secrets in exchange for being able to abduct a few citizens for testing. Apparently, President Eisenhower decided to blow off the warning issued to the United States by the benevolent ET species, in the name of progress.

According to Captain Schneider, The Greada Treaty was the first and only treaty to ever step outside the confines of the Constitution, being signed into action without Congressional ratification. The conditions in the treaty were set down by the U.S. Government: In exchange for advanced technology, the Grays were to provide the government with a list of all abductees. They were then to erase all memory of the abduction trauma from the citizens, and were to return all American citizens unharmed. The abduction list was supposed to be quite small and approved first by the Oval Office. Well, as it always goes when one dominant culture interfaces with a less dominant culture, the Grays didn't deliver all the technology they had promised, disregarded the treaty completely, took as many people as they wanted to, didn't wipe any memories, left people physically impaired, and didn't care about any recourse from the Humans. One could argue the karma involved here, as the U.S. Government broke treaties with countless Native American cultures during the Western Expansion. You'd think they would have seen this one coming.

Starting in 1994, Captain Philip Schneider toured the nation for the following two years, speaking very openly and in great detail about black budgets, underground installments, UFOs, CIA inspired civilian murder and drugs, The Greada Treaty, the Philadelphia Experiment, the UN's involvement in Marshal Law and concentration camps, the New World Order, man-made earthquakes and viruses, and stealth technology.

In 1996, he was found dead in his Willsonville, Oregon apartment.

The Clackamas County Coroner's office ruled Captain Schneider's death a stroke. His ex-wife smelled a rat and implored the funeral home to allow her to view the body, which was badly decomposed. She later received a call from the Clackamas County Detectives, who claimed the funeral director had found something odd. A rubber catheter hose had been stretched three times around Captain Schneider's neck and knotted in the front. The County Medical Examiner ruled Captain Schneider's death a suicide, but his ex-wife thought differently. She recounted a conversation with her very religious ex-husband where he shared that if he ever turned up dead by "suicide" – he'd been murdered. To add to the mystery, nothing was missing from his apartment – no gold, no valuables or electronics – except all of his lecture materials which included information on Alien metals, photographs of UFOs in relation to Operation Crossroad and, most notably, gone were his notes for an upcoming book on the Alien agenda.

That's one heck of a stroke.

Nowadays, the military and the Grays attempt to avoid each other as much as possible, though the military has taken the Gray's minimal technology offerings, along with and their biological research, well to heart. In 2005, a presentation was given at the Pentagon where a scientist displayed new evidence that the VMAT2 gene, one of the 30,000 within the human genome, was responsible for recognizing the human spiritual experience. Called "The God Gene", the scientist hypothesized that by spreading a genetically engineered "vaccine" throughout radically religious populations by attaching it to a common virus, they would target The God Gene and "immunize" religious radicals who have an "over-expression" of the VMAT2 gene. The goal would be to eliminate extreme acts of violence in the name of religion and reduce terrorism in the Middle East. Basically, the scientist proposed a spiritual lobotomy delivered by a virus at a chromosomal level. In the presentation, the scientist explained that they have already used respiratory viruses such as "flu" and "rhino virus" to carry the "immunization" against The God Gene. The name of the project was – and is -- "FunVax", which, the scientist goes on to explain, is in reference to religious FUNdamentalism. Catchy, huh? Google "Pentagon Briefing on Removing the God Gene" for your very own front row seat to this fascinating tribute to Dr. Mengele.

The genetic isolation of the VMAT2 gene is information courtesy of the very curious and very morally questionable Grays -- who are obsessed with our ability to connect to Spirit, and obsessed with genetic manipulation. Just as Nazi Germany snagged countless nuclear secrets from the Grays that we later inherited by inheriting German scientists, we now have The God Gene.

Humanity + Grays = Bad News, which is what our more benevolent OffWorld cousins were trying to tell us back in 1954.

Even the ancient Hopi peoples were aware that we are not alone in the universe, and of all the OffWorlders, Grays were a rotten bunch. Hopi legend recounts that there were two races on the earth -- the Children of the Feather, who originated from the skies, and the Children of the Reptile, who originated from beneath the earth. The Children of the Reptile were also referred to as "Two Hearts", and considered capricious and evil. The legend goes that they had chased the Hopi Indians out from beneath the earth.

According to the Hopi, the U.S.A. has signed a treaty with none other than the Children of the Reptile -- Children of the Serpent, to be exact. They had no idea about the actual Greada Treaty of 1954. Respectively, the Hopi have signed a treaty with the Children of the Feather -- or our more benevolent ET friends. Some even posit that the Children of the Feather are Angels. If you ever needed proof that the government was in bed with the Devil, just ask the Hopi.

Speaking of serpents, now would be a good time to mention that they Grays are said to be a subservient race to a group of ancient warring Reptilian creatures from the hidden tenth planet Niburu that supposedly cuts through our solar system every 3,000 years.

Honestly, I don't know about the whole Niburu thing. But I can tell you that there really is a species of Reptilian OffWorlders, although I think the human term "Reptilian" sounds ridiculous. However, they do look like evil Sleastack, for those of you who remember *The Land of the Lost* on Saturday morning TV. Unlike Sleastack, which walked at a snail's pace and were so ineffective that I could never figure out why Will and Holly would even bother running away from them – I mean, my Granny could have outrun a Sleastack – Reptilians are very tall, agile, and have quite an ego. They're pretty gnarly as OffWorlders go – sort of like the lovechild between a Velociraptor and a Klingon.

Thankfully I haven't had any face to face meetings with these lovelies, but I've accidently snagged an occasional conversation or two out of the ethers as they've passed by interdimensionally while moving very large armadas of captive Beings to somewhere depressing. I try not to stay on their channel too long. If I can see them – they can see me. Archeological evidence left behind from countless ancient cultures worldwide recount the presence of Reptilians: Iguana-Men (Mayans), Dragon Kings (China), the Kappa (Japan), the Naga (India), the Jinn

(Middle East), the Annunaki (Sumeria), and even in the book of Genesis, God punished Eve for her interaction with a Serpent. Though some of these accounts date back nearly 9,000 years and are geographically scattered across the globe, the one startling commonality is the description of how these Reptilian beings interacted with Humanity. Put bluntly, they're either enslaving us in exchange for their "help", or eating us. Or both.

Reptilians consider themselves superior to the race of mutts known as Humanity. (One doesn't have to be human to be a racist.) There are entire cults across the world who are obsessed with this species, believing that the Reptilians are 1) Demonic, 2) Head up the New World Order, 3) Live in Hollow Earth, or 4) Are shape-shifting hybrids posing as world leaders and politicians. I can't say I'm onboard with anything on that list. And, I would be remiss in my duties as your friendly neighborhood Psychic if I didn't confess that I really don't get any actual Psychic confirmation on the whole "Secret Planet Niburu" thing – the planet that supposedly was once part of our solar system, but had been thrown out of orbit due to a collision with another planet that resulted in the other planet's destruction, a fragment of which became Earth. The Niburu yarn is a bit much. It sounds like something Isaac Asimov came up with in a pinch, though it's actually credited to an interpretation of Sumerian mythology. To recap -- yes, there are Reptilians, but no, there is no "Niburu". Conversely, I wouldn't put it past a species as cold and arrogant as the Reptilians to subjugate a less technologically advanced race like the Grays – if nothing else, just for fun, seeing as that the Grays are pretty boring as a species. Boring or not, those two deserve each other.

Most of Humanity has actually interfaced with very kind OffWorlders over the millennia. Yet, those OffWorlders didn't demand that temples be built to them with their logo all over the place, so we don't have as many accounts of our benevolent friends. Whispers of their presence remains with talk of the enlightened populations of Atlantis and Lemuria, or even certain passages in the Bible. Most of the time, I overhear "conversations" from these more benevolent species. I'm prone to believe that the "woman" in my Rubbermaid garbage can "dream" so many years ago was part of the same benevolent species that attempted to give President Eisenhower wise counsel. Rotten ETs don't really interact with me anymore, thanks to the removal of my Official Gray Chakral Hair Net.

There are so many OffWorld species that frequent our planet that explaining all of them would literally lend itself to another book. I can't say that I know from where they all originate, as many of them aren't even of this dimension, yet once they cross into this earth plane – they pop up on my grid, and I've got them. I can tell whether or not they got here by traveling through space as we do, or if they simply poked a hole in space and wormholed their way here. And I can see what their home world looks like by looking through their memories. Yet a vast majority of these species come from "galaxies" that are so different from ours, that are so far away, that I don't even have a reference for how to "point" to their location, given a map of our known Universe. Considering our best attempts at exploring space still result in limited little star maps brought forth from pieces of titanium flailing through the vacuum beyond while beaming back photos on radio waves -- we truly have no way of accounting for their environments. So instead, I have to settle for extracting information on their home worlds, like their culture, how they look at their role in the universe, their technology, and their sociology. Which, of course, is all pretty cool. I just couldn't tell you where to find them: "Climb the mountain on Easter Island, go through the Vortex between two granite slabs when the Ionosphere is activated by a C-Class solar flare or greater, whisk down the wormhole, hang a left at the flickering squiggly, slide down the plasma plunge, take a quick right at the black fold – you'll feel it, you won't see it -- and bingo, you're there."

I think I'll stick to how they think.

Anyway, the "The Atlas of Intergalactic Species" is on my "to do" list before I die. But that's another project for another time. In reference to these chapters, our distant galactic cousins are an ancient race of folks, quite benevolent actually. They not only look a whole lot more like us, though they primarily exist in a body of energy rater than matter, but they had a lot more to do with helping the evolution of humanity along, both technologically and genetically. However, it should be noted that their technological contributions were made responsibly, and a long time ago, assisting ancient peoples to come out of the caves and live with greater ease. This benevolent species is much more interested in working with humanity at humanity's own evolutionary pace, rather than giving us means to shoot hundreds of years past our emotional development with technological advancements. They recognize the folly in placing too much power in the hands of a species that simply has no idea how to wrap their brains around the consequences of such power. Their interest in assisting humanity was, and is, genuine – they are a distant relative of ours, anyway. And just like we'd all step in to help out a younger sibling who was struggling by applying our life experiences–they do the same.

Hold your water, Creationists – God is still in charge of this whole experimental Petri dish down here, so there's no need to wave the Armageddon flags just yet. And please hold the hate mail; I'm not discrediting God by pointing out that God made more than one intelligent species in the universe. In fact, I'm calling God out as prolific.

Speaking of intelligent, all OffWorlders – well, the ones who visit earth, anyway – possess space-time bending technology. Our OffWorld cousins tend to use the temporal doorways such as the Norway Spiral. Intra-dimensional travel is old hat to intergalactic races, all of which have been around much longer than Humanity. There are many versions of this technology spread across many OffWorld cultures. Though we would consider all of them to be rather astounding, there is definitely a pecking order amongst "those races in the know" in which the technology is considered extraordinary. For instance, every car has an engine, but some engines are hybrids, some run on electricity, and some run on gasoline. However, to a Lakota Sioux Tribesman in 1817, even a 1960 Ford Edsel would seem like a crazed miracle of transportation. By OffWorld technological standards, the type of intra-dimensional craft and technology used by the Grays is, in effect – an Edsel.

Edsel or not, I, like the Lakota Tribesman of 1817, found the intra-dimensional "hatch" that opened in my childhood bedroom floor on that bizarre night in Montana back in 1991 – to be astounding. From levitating garbage cans to other-wordly doorways in the shag carpeting, I can proudly and uncomfortably say I was abducted… when abducted wasn't cool.

Sing along if you're old enough to know the tune.

# 8
## POSSESSION: THE SPIRIT NEXT DOOR
### WHERE: TACOMA, WASHINGTON
### LOCATION: HILLTOP

As a Clairvoyant and Medium who has worked in the field for over a decade with private clients, corporate clients, and even law enforcement, there are quite a few tales that I could share that would likely be, at the very least, engaging. However, there is one tale that surpasses engaging, and places itself into the sole position of being harrowing. It is this tale that I shall endeavor to recite, because the circumstances surrounding the tale actually frightened me. And that's tough to do.

On the night of October 23rd, 2010, I had just finished playing a concert at a venue in Tacoma, WA. You see, my other J-O-B is "Rock Star" – no, really, it is – and upon finishing up this concert, two friends who had attended the concert suggested to me that I accompany them back to their home, in order to "check out" the house next door. The reason for this late night inquiry, aside from perhaps too many Hot Toddies during the concert on the part of my friends, was due to the fact that my friends were care-taking this home and they thought it may be haunted.

Well, seeing as that we were a week away from Halloween and seeing as though the ethers are particularly thin during that time of year and seeing as though I, too, had a Hot Toddy in order to chase the damp mossy Northwest air out of my Los Angeles-based bronchial tubes – this all seemed like a very sensible idea at the time.

By the time I was able to get my musical gear packed away, even with the help of the record label staff, it was quite late. We arrived at my friends' home, a turn-of-the-century Victorian in the historic section of Tacoma, and next door sat the target – another turn-of-the-century Victorian with a dark personality, and even darker windows. It was a typical Northwest fall: wet, rainy, dark, and a little miserable – perfect ghost hunting weather.

My friends "Alice" and "Sarah" had a house guest, "Rex", who expressed interest in coming along on our impromptu paranormal investigation. Of course, I knew Rex, and thought it would be fun to have one more person on the ghost hunt. So the four of us trotted off next door in the wind and the rain to get to the bottom of the potential haunting. On the way, Alice told me that while she was next door feeding the cats at this supposedly haunted house, she felt someone upstairs. Naturally, the house was vacant, so that was a bit unsettling for her.

As we neared the house, climbing the corner lot cement stairs that were slick with black moss and time-crumbled edges, the pit of my stomach seized and the hair on my arms began to stand up. That's never a good sign. This place was not only haunted, but haunted with something that was a very negative presence, and was none to happy about my arrival. I didn't say much at this point because I didn't want to alarm anyone, but I did turn to both Alice and Sarah and confirm that yes, Virginia – the house is haunted.

"We haven't even gone in yet," said Sarah.

It was at this point that Rex stood on the moldy, rickety porch of this old Victorian home, and stated very plainly: "I don't want to go in."

Now, at this juncture in our tale, it's very important to point out that Rex is a very lovely, very intelligent, and very gay man. I mean, extremely gay. Rex makes me look like a linebacker, and I mean that with the utmost respect for linebackers. So, upon Rex's protest, which came out sounding a bit like Jim J. Bullock throwing a fit on Hollywood Squares, I naturally dismissed the incident, told Rex to buck up, and all four of us entered the house.

It was more like walking into a vacuum.

The place was thick with spiritual occupation, sickness, and secrets. And none of them were good. The house was done up in dark antique woods. It smelled of rotting drapes and cat boxes. Rex's eyes popped wide open and he made an effort to return to the porch. However, Sarah talked him into staying, and onward we strode into the living area, which was a hodgepodge of mismatched furniture and scarred wooden floors. Not only was this home haunted by at least one very unhappy occupant, but by 1970s linoleum which had been slapped atop painted floors in the dining room.

I could feel this entity hiding, seething at me from the ethers. It was a tall male in his mid-forties with a long beard and mutton chops, no moustache, and a balding head – the kind that would beg for a comb-over if only this man had lived in 1963. The bald head-mound was surrounded by a tangled nest of stringy salt and pepper hair that fell to his shoulders. He had bulging slate colored eyes which he held overly-wide open under bushy eyebrows, and a blue naval-looking coat adorned with brass buttons done up to his neck. He was a nasty person and he smelled, even in death.

As Mediums do, I was pulling energetic information from him, and as spirits on the defensive do, he was downloading information from me. It was a race to see who could find a chink in the other person's armor first. I began to relay to my friends who I was in contact with: This man was an abuser. He didn't believe in God. He didn't believe in anything but his own ability to rule his home, which he had once done with an iron fist. He had a rage within him that permeated the atmosphere of the home like a depressive blanket. I wondered who ever could have dwelled in this house from day to day without falling ill.

"The man who lives here is in the hospital with stage four cancer," answered Sarah. "That's why we are here feeding the cats."

Well, there you have it.

Rex had tried to leave several times, but I convinced him to stay, because I could see that this spirit didn't like having all of us there, and with a spirit who was this bent on being aggressive, there was safety in numbers. Just as the malevolent spirit man would hiss something awful at me through the ethers, Rex would say, "He doesn't like you."

Rex could hear him, too. I began to re-think Rex's Paul Lynde protests about being in the home. To my utter surprise, Rex was a Medium.

I pulled Sarah into the foyer of the home, out of earshot, and said, "Why didn't you tell me that Rex was an open channel?"

"Because I didn't know," she answered. "I don't think he knows, either."

This was not a good situation. Rex, though an incredibly sweet guy, was not a small guy, at six feet four inches tall. He also had more than a few cocktails in his system after an evening out, and now he was smack in the middle of one of the more haunted homes I'd been in with one of the more nasty entities I'd encountered in awhile. I returned to the living room and asked Rex if he wanted to leave, but he was fine to stay, and he went to sit by Sarah for moral support.

At one point, this spirit man was yelling obscenities at me – keep in mind, this dead guy hated women – and he demanded to be called by name. I wasn't terribly concerned with his demands, but he kept shoving a "C" surname at me, so I finally relented, thinking I could at least have a conversation with him and talk him into crossing over, which would have been a fool's errand considering this gem of a once-human didn't even believe in God. But a girl has to try.

I couldn't quite get the name, and I was saying, "I'm sorry, are you saying Connel? Is your name Connel?"

Suddenly, from the corner, a slumped over Rex, eyes closed, bellowed in a deep and un-Rex voice: "COLONEL! YOU CALL ME COLONEL!"

There was a quiet in the room that was more uncomfortable than the acrid smell of the cat boxes. Sarah, who was standing by Rex, froze with her panicked gaze trained on me. Alice was seated across the room at the kitchen table, and simply stared. I'd known Rex for years, and never heard that booming deep voice come out of him – until now.

The situation had gone from "not good" to "dangerous". Rex was a big fellow, and he was no longer driving his own ship. The Colonel had pushed his way into Rex and taken up occupancy. A Medium who is not in control of his or her aptitudes is much like a swinging door on an old saloon – anyone can come in, and anyone can go out. Without knowing how to "latch the door", a Medium is at risk for a spiritual squatter. Rex had the worst kind of squatter possible: a victimizer who had remained physically impotent in death for over 100 years and was itching for a fight.

"What's happening?" Sarah asked, her voice shaking.

"Rex isn't home right now," I answered flatly, attempting to remain calm as I continued to systematically pull The Colonel's file out of the ethers, frantic to find something to leverage against this entity that would force it to leave Rex's body. The information coming back to me wasn't helping. Yes, The Colonel hated women. He had raped both his wife and his daughter repeatedly throughout their lives, finally killing the daughter when she was in her mid-teens when he accidently choked her to death during a sexual assault. The daughter's remains had been buried on the property in an unmarked grave that was beneath the floor of the dining room, right under the very spot I was standing. This was one sick muther-effer, now possessing a six foot four male frame.

The only "edge" that I had was in The Colonel's difficulty in attempting to maneuver Rex's body. It had been a long time since The Colonel had the weight of gravity pulling upon him. I had to figure out how to drive out this crazy dead old nut before The Colonel had full use of Rex's bulky flesh suit. The race was on.

The Colonel slumped off the chair where Rex was seated and pulled himself across the floor like a drunken Golem, all the way to Alice, who was still seated at the table. Alice was a bit numb over all this, and the Colonel tried to climb up the back of the chair and scare her by saying some unsavory things, but Alice didn't react. She knew better than to feed into this entity's rage.

"You need to leave this house. You're dead," I said sternly.

"YOU DON'T KNOW ANYTHING ABOUT MY HOUSE!" The Colonel bellowed.

Sarah was panicked, trying to help by saying, "You need to leave Rex alone. That's not your body."

Of course, The Colonel just laughed, and I erupted into goose bumps, because the laugh was so foreign to Rex's vocal chords. I was just putting together the thought in my mind that I would pull the dead daughter card – try and take the power away from this abuser by exposing a secret – when The Colonel began pounding the dining room floor, over and over again, laughing with a guttural rasp that made my eyes water. I couldn't control the absolutely stone-cold sensation rushing up my back. He had pulled my thoughts straight from my head and beat me to the punch, slapping the spot on the floor where beneath, he had interned his daughter's remains. In doing so – he completely creeped me out.

Score: One for The Colonel, Zero for Danielle.

Thoughts are energy, ripe for the picking. Whatever he knew, I knew. But whatever I knew, he knew. Thus is the coup in spiritual work. I quickly realized that I needed to come up with something that would throw him off his game. The Colonel was a masochist, all about the control. I would have to knock him off his center before he pulled my next greatest fear straight out of my head, and acted it out.

I looked down at the dining room floor where I could "see" his daughter's discombobulated skeleton, twisted in the crawlspace dirt below the linoleum. God, I hated that linoleum. All gold, maroon, and brown, it was the finest 1972 had to offer. I went with it. "If you know so much about your own house, why did you let someone put this god-awful linoleum down?"

The Colonel began to writhe, and a dismayed growling sound emitted from the back of his throat, but he did not respond. Excellent! I continued on. "I mean, look at this garbage. It's hideous! Who lets someone come into their house and put this horrendous crap on their hardwood? What kind of moron let's someone ruin their floors?"

The Colonel growled a little louder, and stammered out, "You don't know anything!"

I could feel the entity reeling over the concept of linoleum, which kept him in his own head and out of mine long enough for me to play the trump card in this poker game.

"And look at you," I continued, "what are you going to do? You've possessed a gay man! That body you're in is queer. He has sex with other men. He's a woman. You're nothing but a sissy, sitting on the floor. No one is afraid of you."

Now, let me take this opportunity to explain that I, as a gay woman, don't think that gay men are sissies, or girls. The Colonel, however, did, which was why I chose the verbiage, straight out of his head. The Colonel took a moment to actually survey the consciousness of the body he had possessed, and for the first time, opened up Rex's eyes wide and in horror. The Colonel was a complete and utter homophobe.

Bingo.

The Colonel began scooting himself into the kitchen, sliding backwards on Rex's bum, dragging his leg. Obviously, the Colonel had been wounded in a battle of some kind, and held onto the consciousness of this injury well into death. He stopped and peered at me from around a cabinet, one lone piercing eye wide open in terror – terror of being emasculated, terror or being crippled, terror of being dead. The terror was hollow, and one of the most chilling things I have ever witnessed.

"You either get up and come at me, or recede," I demanded.

The Colonel continued to drag himself into the kitchen. I took advantage of the situation and rushed in, squatting next to Rex with my hand on his chest. "Rex, come on, buddy. Come out. Push forward. Wake up."

Since Rex had no idea how to use his abilities, I had no idea what his key phrase would be. Most Mediums have a key phrase they recognize so if they are possessed past their ability to control the spirit, the phrase can be uttered and rattle their native consciousness into kicking out the secondary spiritual squatter. I had no idea what would appeal to Rex, but I could feel The Colonel running away, back into the recesses of this dank old house. At the end of the day, The Colonel was nothing more than a coward.

Rex blinked and looked at me, then looked up at Sarah from his spot on the floor. "Oh dear, girls, did I fall down? Too many martinis?"

Rex was back online.

We didn't explain what had happened to him at that moment, as Rex had absolutely no recollection of what had occurred. Sarah mentioned he had scooted himself into the kitchen, and Rex didn't believe us. We finally got him on his feet and went to leave the house. As we were leaving, Rex began to fuss, wanting to stay. Often times, when a person is possessed by another entity, the person will maintain the emotional responses of the entity for awhile, until they can consciously flush them out. Rex started to get a rather glazed look in his eye as we approached the foyer. We quickly scooted him outside and locked the door behind him.

On the porch, he began to panic, wanting back into the house. Sarah was firm about him returning home next door, and I distracted him with conversation about shoes and belts, long enough to get him down the rickety front stairs and onto the main sidewalk below. I had one arm, Sarah had his other arm, and Alice walked behind him, making sure he would not bolt back for the home. Rex twisted his head backwards, looking up at the old tattered Victorian, saying: "Girls, I want to go back in the house."

The rest of the night involved me, Alice and Sarah attempting to explain to Rex what had happened. Rex didn't believe us, or rather, didn't want to accept what had happened to him ("I don't believe in all that hoo-doo!") until finally at one point during the evening, he broke down crying, unable to even put into words the horrendous sexual atrocities that "he" had envisioned acting out on me, Sarah, and Alice. Considering that Rex is the gayest man alive, those thoughts must have been exceptionally traumatic on a number of levels.

I had to explain to him that the thoughts he had left in his consciousness were (obviously) not his own, but that of The Colonel, like old paint left on the side of the can in which it was once packaged. I worked energetically on Rex to rid him of the rest of the negative residual garbage that The Colonel had left behind in him, and discussed with him how to properly use his spiritual gifts.

Working with one's spiritual gifts is not for everybody. I made a key error in judgment that night in goading someone to stay in a haunted location when they clearly wanted to leave. Though I didn't know that Rex was a Medium, I did pick up that he was spiritually sensitive, and I should have honored his instinct to remove himself from the situation. I mistook his actual worry over the situation for the musings of a natural born drama queen. In my mild defense, if you knew Rex – you'd see how this would've been an easy mistake to make. However, even Rex with his colorful mannerisms would not have been able to concoct an "act" like the one we had all witnessed.

In over a decade of doing this kind of work in the field, I've never watched a full-body possession occur, especially when dealing with a human entity. I honestly believed that non-authorized full-body possessions were saved for demonic cases. All of the Mediums and Channels that I have ever worked with, myself included, have a great deal of experience in disallowing unwanted entities from occupying their bodies, so the thought of a "ghost" entering a person's body with such force was never an issue to consider.

The experience with Rex was incredibly unnerving and struck a chord with me. It drove home the fact that what we do out in the field as Psychics and Mediums is truly dangerous if not handled properly. Spirit life has the potential to harm certain people who are more susceptible to spiritual frequencies. This is necessarily true if the person who is dealing with the phenomenon is not well versed in what they are doing or doesn't know what they are capable of. The sobering truth was that we, all four of us, got out of that house unscathed — on a miracle. The situation involving a wide-open Medium without any discernment skills, so many Hot Toddies, and a masochistic negative entity, should have been much worse. However, The Universe cut us a break that night.

You know the saying "God takes pity on drunks and fools"? Well, I guess we double qualified that evening.

Rex promised me that he would look into developing his Medium abilities, as he clearly is a very gifted and wide-open channel who could potentially help many people with such a pure spiritual aptitude. But I know that since the incident, he has steered clear of any sort of spiritual environments or pursuits. His last words:

"Honey, all this hoo doo is a little too much for little ol' me."

# 9
# DEMONS IN THE BASEMENT
## WHERE: MONTGOMERY HOUSE BED AND BREAKFAST
## LOCATION: KALAMA, WASHINGTON

One of the most unsettling types of entities to deal with would be Demons, and perhaps not for the reasons one would expect. Many think of Demons as red-hoofed tormentors that growl in the darkness and spit at priests. But in fact, they are much more subtle than that. Demons are the ultimate sociopathic predator. They are chaos for the sake of chaos in a way that we, as human beings, are simply incapable of understanding, even on our most "evil" days. And, like a predator, Demons aren't going to simply rush out into the light, for all to see. That's a trait reserved for a human spirit – the need to be noticed.

Like a stealthy undercover operative, Demons don't want to be noticed, unless it's on their schedule. Instead, like a predator, they will stalk their prey from the shadows, silently, logging everything about us – what scares us, when we are weak -- decoding everything about their prey for later use. They prefer to execute an attack over time. The longer the attack drags on, the better, designed for maximum suffering. They are patient, and they are nasty, and they have no conscience whatsoever. Imagine the perfect sociopath with super-hero Psychic abilities, the patience of Job, all the time in the world, and a penchant for very long term suffering: Hannibal Lecter meets *Saw*.

It's not very often that one encounters Demons, and people who are not experienced in the field tend to mistake certain Elementals as Demons. This is because some Elementals can be really nasty, and look like they crawled right up out of hell. However, Demons are their own insidious creatures, made from dark to return to darkness, and once you've dealt with them, you don't forget their resonance, or the experience.

Unlike Elementals, which are generally bound to an area in the ground, as it's their job to "gate keep" that area of the earth, Demons are drawn to suffering and to pain. Elementals are God's nature-keepers, "green middle-management" of sorts, and are much more interested in chasing people off land that they feel will be jeopardized by human occupation. With Elementals, the land – not the people – is the priority. Demons want to keep people around because they "eat" the energy we give off when we suffer. We become a food source for these creatures in our deepest agony. They are the worst of the worst when it comes to spiritual infestations. They attempt to trap us in our own fear indefinitely so they may continue to eat us alive, like cattle stalled in pens.

I have nothing positive at all to say about Darkness, or about Demons.

Dealing with Demons is an exercise in mind-over-fear. It's an exercise in faith. To deal with Demons in a physical location means to first deal with one's own Demons within. The exercise is to center oneself so wholeheartedly in God, and in Light, that nothing – and I mean *nothing* – that these creatures toss at you will be seen as "real". And believe me -- they only hit below the belt.

To prep for dealing with Demons, think *Kung Fu* meets Yoda. As everything in life, Demons, too, have their shortfalls, and as such, have "chinks" in their armor. To deal with these entities, one must keep a steady focus on their weak spots. For instance, one can always count on a Demon to try and scare you. Knowing that, if you are aware of what scares you, you can control your response to the fear. Demons "eat" fear, and just like milking a cow, they frighten us to extract their "nutrient" from our reaction. Like chumming the ocean with blood off the coast of South Africa – fear is their dinner bell, and here come great white sharks.

For as old and as crafty as they are, Demonic life is very predictable in how it will attack. Knowing this gives a person a leg up on the "stages" of the battle. The ace in the hole is God. Demons are born of Darkness. They never were human, and their energy oscillates at a lower vibration than that of Light. Humankind originates from Light. Even though we only contain one teensy tiny spark of God within the human soul, it is enough to "transmit" a "greater broadcast" coming from God

Itself,. Turn that broadcast in the direction of the Demon, and watch them scatter.

Spiritual Light oscillates at a very high frequency, so in terms of physics, the faster a particle vibrates, the faster it travels. The faster a particle travels, the more "excited" it can make other particles, shaking apart any matter in its path that exists on a lower vibration. Think of how Ultra Sonic waves are used in washing machines – they vibrate out the dirt on a molecular level because the dirt molecules don't vibrate as fast as they do. When we call on the Power of God (channeling high-vibration energy), and "step out of the way" to allow that power to radiate through us. "Stepping out of the way" means we get a handle on our own fear and release the ego that would convince us *we* are what Demons fear. Nothing is further from the truth. They don't fear us. They fear our "fire hose of Light" effect. We must remain calm, focus, and douse these dark pests in a wall of Light that is akin to pouring salt on a slug. Which one should never do.

The slug, I mean.

Think of vampire lore -- how vampires explode when a stake is driven through their heart. That's more the immediate effect of the high vibration of Light hitting the low vibration of Darkness. The latter doesn't stand a chance, and these Demons are well aware of this. They will flee rather than be blown apart by the power – or the vibration – of God. As such, they will do everything they can to distract us from turning on that fire hose. It's a battle of wills, and the less personal one makes an encounter with a Demon, the better. If we as humans continue to fall prey to our fears in dealing with these pests, then we can't remain calm enough to get our head around stepping out of our own way, to direct the Light of God right at these nasties.

They hate that, and not in their "love to hate" sort of way.

I refer to Demons as "pests" because put into their proper context, and all their spooky party tricks aside – that's exactly what they are. No more, no less. Demons don't want us to realize this handy fact. It really does take the wind out of their "spooky sails". And, considering it is in their ability to frighten us that their power lies, demystifying these pests then becomes a major Demon buzz-kill.

Though they can be a pain to get rid of and can have some health side effects, just like other pests such as cockroaches which spread disease, Demons are nothing more than an inconvenient infestation. The more Human Kind can get our minds around this fact – the less power these entities have in this incarnation. They're vermin, like mice, secretly scurrying for kitchen crumbs while trying to set up shop under the darkness of our stove.

"Crumbs" in Demon terms amount to the energy created by human suffering. Since pain is a food source for these pests, Demons are attracted to areas in which great traumas have occurred. These High Pain Portals are a Demon buffet. Lower rank Demons (and yes, there are "ranks" within Demonic structure, just as there are ranks in our Angelic realm) tend to hover around mental institutions, where the distress of poor mentally ill people erupts like a disturbed chocolate fountain into the ethers. This is the main reason that abandoned mental institutions still have dark, Demonic figures lurking about. The energy that erupts off of a person in distress will store in surroundings for an indefinite amount of time. Depending on geographic features of the area and the very materials used to build a structure in which the pain occurred, distress can remain trapped in a physical location for hundreds, if not thousands of years. Paranormal Investigators call this phenomenon a Residual Haunting.

Vortexes can also open a pathway for Demonic life, as Demons don't care to work too hard for anything. A Vortex doesn't always mean a Demon is present – in fact, more Interdimensionals, Elementals, and OffWorlders (Extraterrestrials) take advantage of Vortex doorways for handy travel than do Demons. But if a Vortex exists over an area that is near pain, the Demonic Life will take advantage of such an entryway and pop through the on their way to the Suffering Cafe.

Dealing in Demonic infestations is not for everyone, and in truth, I deal with this area of the paranormal as little as possible. Not because I fear Demons, because I don't -- in spite of their innate creepiness. It's more that the hassle of dealing with them is an enormous inconvenience. I don't want to worry about "tracking" their diseases back into my own environment. Like someone who works for the CDC, when one deals with Demons, one must wear a suit – only the suit is made of Light and Will. However, like working for the CDC, one may accidently track through Ebola and inadvertently march the poison through the grocery store on the way home. Then you have a real hayride on your hands. However, with proper preparation, dealing with Demons is much like fumigating rather than quarantine. Instead of covering one's eyes and lungs, one must protest the spirit and the mind.

So.

Since these entities are masters at maniacal fear tactics; since they view us as an unintelligent food source; since they don't forge emotional attachment to the outcome of any situation in which we are involved --

intelligently interacting with human beings is not high on their priority list. They'd rather just eat the vibes coming off of our goose bumps. Let's face it – how many of us want to have a conversation with a chicken? Or a cow? We look at these creatures like something that we cultivate to eat. So Demons view humanity. They don't care about engagement. They care about causing suffering so they can eat. Only when they run out of party tricks from the shadows -- feelings of oppression, paranoia, sudden domestic violence -- do they take interacting with humanity to the next level. And that's when we, as human beings, have the opportunity to hose them down.

It takes a special location to stage a good Demon hose-down. They must feel confident enough in their ability to draw power from their surroundings in order to engage a human being. All the pieces of the puzzle must be in place. If a location is already prone to Vortexes, thinning ethers, and sits atop ground where atrocities have been committed and great pain is then stored – then you've got yourself a Demon roach motel. Occupancy, and attitude, will be high.

Just like at Montgomery House Bed and Breakfast in Kalama, WA.

Montgomery House sits atop two underground streams that cross one another, creating a natural vortex. Through this doorway, a litany of spirit life crosses in and out, making the Bed and Breakfast a haunted highway. In fact, one of the streams trickled right into the home itself, a live spring in the basement. This home is also roughly 100 yards from the mighty churning Columbia River, and was built in 1908 upon granite bedrock heavy in iron. So the Bed and Breakfast is a geophysical ghost trap.

Add to this fact that Montgomery House used to be a hospital, then a Bordello, then a Bordello with a "doctor's clinic" downstairs (to take care of unwanted pregnancies in the late 20's) and, well, you have something that really is the distressed energy backdrop for the home in AMC's *American Horror Story*.

Only Montgomery House is real.

I chose to film my paranormal documentary about this location, because I've really never before happened upon a more perfect representation of geophysical and emotional attributes that created a haunting of such magnitude (thus the portion of the film's title, *The Perfect Haunting*).I felt a need to document this environment. It had everything: Human ghosts from different time periods, Residual Hauntings, Elementals, and in the basement -- Demons.

I mean, really?

The Demons were going to be the challenge, not only to get rid of, but to engage on any level. Though Demons work to stay as hidden as possible in order to achieve maximum torment results, they emit a dead give-away that they simply cannot hide. It's in their very resonation, their footprint, and no matter how hard they try – it's their tip-off.

Like a skunk has a stink -- Demons have oppression.

You can feel the prohibitive dread hanging thick in the air on your chest when these entities are nearby, making it hard to even breathe. It's not the same kind of "hair raising on the back of your head" goose-bumpy feeling that human spirits will instill in a person, due to all the EMF (Electro Magnetic Fields) in the air. Demons don't even emit EMF if they don't want to, because they aren't the same kind of spiritual make-up that we are. They are a completely separate energy, born of a different incarnation and dimension, and it resonates at such a low level. In its native format, Demonic energy is not even on our "instrument detection charts". Aside from a lack of electronically detectable energy traces, Demons will *always* trigger the human spirit's alarm thanks to their unmistakable oppression.

See, we humans have all sorts of built-in spiritual protection devices that we are barely aware of. We take for granted our spiritual wiring. Since we can't often detect Demons with a typical ghost-hunting EMF meter -- though once in awhile, one will throw out a lot of EMF either because it tripped a geophysical attribute tied to the location, or on purpose, just to throw a paranormal investigator off track -- we as human have to rely strongly on our "spiritual catfish whiskers".

Or, as it's more commonly known: our gut.

There was no mistaking my gut feeling when I stood in the kitchen at Montgomery House, eyeballing that narrow five panel antique door leading down to the basement. That door, though pristinely painted white, had a way of staring right through you. It reminded me of that one weirdo at a bar who downs too much Maker's Mark and glares you down all night, mistaking you in the whiskey haze for a filet mignon dinner. I would enter the renovated kitchen of Montgomery House to retrieve a cup of coffee in the morning and go out of my way to avoid making eye contact with that petite, narrow door. One would think that would be easy considering the door didn't have eyes. What waited on the other side, however – did.

The door itself had the energy of an open axe wound that had been made up to look like a beauty queen. It was forced and macabre, and to add to the general creepy vibe, the door had a rickety lock on the kitchen side, to prevent something from below from opening it up. It was a pittance of a lock, one of those jangly hook-and-eye things set quite high. That even made it creepier. I suppose it could be argued that this little weenie lock was a security measure, as in the basement there was a door that lead to the outside, letting out right under the teetering porch. Perhaps the lock was the last sentry to detour would-be prowlers from entering the home. But in truth, the lock seemed more like a placebo, as one swift pull of that door from the other side would rip that tiny hook eyelet right out of the dry antique wood in which it had been crookedly screwed.

It was time for me to address the basement. The basement had been reaching out to me since I arrived at the location, and I had been ignoring it. In fact, during a pre-shoot meeting in the main floor parlor with one of the homeowners, I had just started discussing my desire to investigate the basement, and as if on cue, the floor beneath our feet BOOMED three times, as if a giant with an enormous fist punched the floorboards from below. I watched as candles on the table rattled, and one of the pictures on the wall hopped a bit from the plaster. A hush fell over the room. The homeowner at the time just stared at me, as I stared at her. She broke the odd tension by laughing and said, "Well, I guess they know you're here."

Living in Southern California, I have an app on my Blackberry that allows me to check the latest seismic activity, up to the second it's reported. (The app is sort of like carrying an umbrella in your briefcase if you live in New York.) The day the floor BOOMED beneath our feet, I made sure to immediately check the seismic records to see if there had been a perfectly timed earthquake anywhere in the Kalama area that day.

No geothermal activity had occurred. The basement was just soured by what lived there.

What dwelled in the basement was attracted to what happened in the home, and on the land. At one point, when the home was a Bordello, it was reported that a "doctor's clinic" would perform turn of the century abortions in the back room of the house. The remains of the fetuses were believed to have been discarded in the basement. I picked up on this energy prior to my knowledge of the home being a Bordello. It was a palpable energy signature that, if you're wired like I am – you just can't miss. In fact, one of the townspeople, who, on a walkthrough of the home while having a "girls night out" with one of the homeowners, had picked up an unmistakable feeling of deceased little children in the basement. This woman hardly considered herself a Psychic -- that's just how thick this energy hung in the ethers When I pressed her during an interview for the film to expand on what she meant by "deceased children", she actually used the word "abortion". I told her that I, too, had picked up on that very same energy, yet had told no one. She flushed red with horror on camera.

The poor woman.

I came to find out later in the filming that the homeowners, while strengthening the home's handmade foundation, came across numerous bones in the basement's dirt floor. The bones had been chopped, sawed, and discarded in the dirt. While renovating the back porch right off the basement, they again encountered piles and piles of bones, yet this time the piles included partial craniums of what looked like tiny human skulls. A determination was never made about the origin of the bones, as the homeowners were on a deadline to complete the construction in order to open for business. In good faith they invited a friend whose background was in archaeology to take a look at the bones, and it was decided that they had come from a cow. Both the homeowners did not agree on this assessment, as one homeowner couldn't reconcile the small craniums and other small bones as "coming from a cow". Yet the pressure to open the business drove the matter of the bones back into the dirt. From there the topic stayed buried, until we started filming.

For the filming, we were going to be spending a lot of time in the basement of Montgomery House. It was one of the most wounded areas of the home, and it didn't help that the basement looked like the set from *Texas Chainsaw Massacre*: dirt floors, low-hanging ceiling beams made from creosote-soaked railroad ties twisted thick with dusty spider webs decorated with dangling mummies of yesteryear's monster arachnids, old locked cabinetry from the turn of the century with God-only-knows-what entombed inside, racks of abandoned lumber bristling with rusted nails and haphazardly tossed onto shelves to create a canyon of avalanching death, live Brown Recluse spiders peering out with eight glistening eyes from between cans of old paint, and the rusting carcass of an old sawdust boiler, it's octopus-legged ducting forever amputated at it's body. The old defunct boiler stood as a sentry in front of a granite grotto nestled in the far corner of the basement. It was through this grotto where one of the underground streams burst into the home, flowing live. Like saliva dripping down the epiglottis of a hungry carnivorous cave, a trickle of water echoed from the gaping black depths -- the only indication the spring was there.

Rob Zombie's set designer could not have created a Demon den with a more eerie flair.

It was time. Upon opening the basement door, I clicked on the light in the stairwell, a dim and dusty bare bulb dangling above my head. The wall of oppression raced up the bare wooden stairs and sucked the breath from my lungs. In fact, the oppression was so bad that I couldn't even stand within a three foot radius of the door without a splitting headache pounding my head apart. And it wasn't just me. The other Sensitive who I requested "weigh in" on the location also  reported a stabbing headache the moment she saw the door open on her computer screen during a webcam walkthrough of the home, 900 miles away.

I'm all for a challenge. but this was not going to be fun. In fact, my Second Unit Director didn't want to wear his headphones while filming in the basement, for fear of hearing a live-time EVP (electronic voice phenomenon) that would freak him out completely. That was a wise choice, as later the footage yielded several incidents where his name was being called by an unearthly voice. My Director of Photography was so nervous about endeavoring into the basement for the investigations that two nights prior to the basement shoot, he attempted to quell his nerves with shots of tequila and whatever else the town bar had on hand. This self-medicating spree resulted in a late night, fog-encrusted vomiting round in the front yard.

Sidebar: He awakened the next day after four hours of sleep to pull off a wonderful 16 hour shoot day consisting of intensive interviews. Yet I digress.

I stood atop the stairs. I was with the home's owner at the time, staring down into this nightmarish pit, and I was wondering how I was going to tell her that her basement was a hole to hell, full of ...one? Two? Three...wait. Four Demons?

Are you kidding me?

I could feel them from the top of the stairs, slithering beneath the staircase and backing into the recesses of the home's dirt foundation, in response to me "feeling" into them. It's not that they were afraid of me. It's that they wanted to make themselves known on their time, not mine.

Typical, for this type of "ambush predator".

To my relief, the home's owner knew that "something" was off with her basement. She turned to me and mentioned that she had always experienced a feeling of dread every time she had opened that door. I can't imagine she wouldn't. It was really horrible.

Upon glancing down, I saw an apparition form at the bottom of the staircase. I couldn't see its head because the ceiling was so low that it blocked the view above its neck. But the apparition was wearing a white turn-of-the-century shirt with narrow blue pinstripes and some sort of extremely heavy black oiled leather or rubber butcher's apron. His hands and forearms were covered in bulky black rubber or leather gloves that crested over his elbows. The apparition stepped forward and put his hand up, as if to say "stop." It was right around this time that the home owner told me that she often experienced the feeling of "get out" or "stay out" at the top of the stairs.

I could see why. Literally.

I wasn't comfortable sharing with her what I was hearing, as this entity was rattling off a list of profanities and insults that made a 50 Cent song sound like the soundtrack to Elmo. So instead I closed the door, and mentioned that there was some nasty energy there. She agreed.

We later went downstairs to the basement with a friend of the homeowner's, who showed up during the filming of the home's walkthrough. We thought we'd check it out with another person onboard. I informed the Director of Photography that we were heading downstairs, and he was none too happy. (That wasn't supposed to happen for another night or so, you see.) Yet down we went. Descending the stairs was like having someone tie rocks to your ankles then throw you in a deep pool – you sink too quickly, and the pressure of the water weighs heavily upon your chest, pressing uncomfortably into your ears. That's exactly how this environment felt, and was a dead-give-away marker for a common paranormal phenomenon: Vortexes. I realized upon descending that not only was I going to be dealing with more than one Demonic entity below, along with the physical affects of the oppression that surrounds them, but I would be dealing with a barometric pressure change. I realized there were several open Vortexes there, likely due to the open spring in the basement crossing over the top of another underground water source. These Vortexes were going to make dealing with Demons difficult. Open Vortexes are a doorway where pests can scatter out easily if the going gets tough. The trick is to have them trapped. When they're cornered, hose them down with Light. That's a lot tougher when they can run out a secret back door.

This was looking like a mess, one creaking stair at a time.

The old chipped plaster stairwell was tight and claustrophobic, and the Demonic oppression made the air feel sticky with dread. From a psychological standpoint, I really hated the fact that the staircase was open backed, just slats of wood on two long runners. In theory, anything could "reach through" the stairs from the inkiness below and grab your ankles from behind. Now, I realized immediately that I needed to banish all thoughts of this from my consciousness, lest our Demonic friends pull my Fear File and, well – grab my ankles from behind through the stairwell, which would inevitably result in me instantly peeing my pants. Always one to be humbled by vanity, I immediately re-routed this imagery into a place of satire, like a scene from *A Christmas Story*.

My struggle with my own psyche had begun.

When we reached the dirt below, I could hear the sickly trickle of the spring from under the granite outcropping in the back of the basement. As is common in Demon-occupied areas, as well as Vortex areas, the ethers are thicker and heavier. As such, the several lights at the bottom of the stairs lost their reach as the darkness sucked their luminosity dry, leaving the back of the basement where the spring trickled in total darkness, even in the face of several hundred watt bulbs. It never ceases to amaze me how dimensional physics affect electromagnetic energy, affecting something as basic as physical light.

I could feel these three…wait, no – four entities crawling up the walls in the back, dragging across the floor, most curious to see what human buffet had clacked down the stairs. Two looked like flattened black slugs, no features but around five feet long and a few feet wide, slithering around the low rafters and through the dirt, occasionally a stick-skinny arm with three long fingers jutting out of the tarry mass to grasp a crossbeam to continue their progression forward. The other two looked like a cross between a faceless, mortally burned monkey and Golem from Lord of the Rings, blacker than the surrounding blackness that swallowed them. These two clung to the back walls while the others progressed.

They were a touch surprised that I clocked all four of them, yet as is common for Demonic life, they certainly weren't intimidated by me. However, I did notice that they kept their distance. I could feel them sizing me up, and I could feel a few twinges of instant repulsion toward the Light in which I choose to align. Though formidable, I recognized them to be lesser Demons on the food chain – the kind that would hang out at a sanatorium in the 1800's and poke some poor chained-up schizophrenic with an invisible psychologically terrifying stick. I didn't like them, and they didn't like me. We were having an Old West standoff, they in their black cowboy hats, and me in my white beaver Stetson. At least we knew where we stood with one another.

The camera was rolling. Though a bare overhead bulb dangled illuminated, I grabbed a flashlight so the camera could better "see". The Demonic ether in the room sucked the light from the air. (Another common side effect of an infestation of this nature is a "dark haze" in a room or space.) I cast the flashlight under the stairs so at least the Director of Photography had something to film. The moment I did, all four of these entities slammed together to create a nightmarish site visible to me through the open steps of the dusty staircase.

It was a girl in her early teens, from the turn of the century judging by her clothes -- dirty as if someone had kept her prisoner in the filth here below. She was floating, still, dead weight hanging several inches from the floor. The flashlight created shadows through the stairs that cut her image with dark stripes. Her dusty black eyelet boot tips hung limply as she hovered, suspended. Her skirts were shredded and caked in dried blood that stained the insides of her petticoats. Her hair was matted, patchy on her scalp where the hair had been torn out, replaced with dirtied scabs. And her face -- was blank. Not in expression, but in content. She had no face at all, and this was the most terrifying.

Score one for the Demon brigade: One of my biggest childhood fears was anything without a face. I had forgotten about such a strange and unfounded fear until it stood in front of me. The girl's arms reached out, her filthy fingers slowly curling as if she was kneading the pain out of the air.

Then she shot straight at me through the stairs.

This was incredibly startling and I sidestepped to avoid a collision with this floating horror. Of course, the camera was not seeing what I was seeing. The camera could only watch as I hopped out of the way.

Great.

The ghoulish "girl" then retreated to the black corner of the basement, right in front of the trickling spring. I followed her with the flashlight, which did nothing to illuminate her but did succeed in casting a blue glow across the weeping granite grotto to her back.

She then proceeded to morph, churning into an unrecognizable mass of disgust that would occasionally take on a form I could recognize: small children missing limbs, deformed and dismembered fetuses, conjoined twins who shared one head with two deformed faces both shrieking in piercing misery – it was a scene from *Jacobs Ladder* meets *Phantasm*.

Though this display was shockingly awful, it was a touch obvious. In its overkill, I was eventually a bit relieved, like when you're watching a scary movie and all of a sudden you're taken out of the frightening moment when you realize, "Wow. That blood looks really fake." Demons often don't know when to dial it back. That which is our strength is also our greatest weakness.

When these Demons realized they weren't going to get any further reaction from me, they disbanded into four black masses and disappeared into the recesses of the basement.

As for the camera? Well, we got a lot of footage of me squatting on the floor, near speechless. The Demons knew exactly what they were doing -- that I could see them and the camera could not. They knew this would cause me frustration.

Score two for the Demon brigade:

I went ahead and excused myself upstairs as I had an enormous headache from the oppressive Vortex pressure in the basement. I said a prayer of blessing as I went up and I made a decision not to tell the homeowner what I'd witnessed down there. Those folks still had to live there, and besides – the goal was to get rid of these Demons before the film crew left, not provide them with another platform to terrorize the family.

I was determined to rid that basement of those nasty pests. I'd invited the holy person and chief from the Cowlitz Indian Tribe to come bless the house, as it sat on former Cowlitz land. This holy man was also a retired United Methodist minister. I was looking forward to hitting the Chaos Crew downstairs with a double whammy.

Several nights of investigations ensued. We coordinated the shoot with a local paranormal group who had interest in investigating Montgomery House. They volunteered to investigate while we were shooting the documentary. Members of the group took turns down in the pitch-black basement, infrared cameras exposing their plight in the dark. While on break upstairs, we were all discussing the nature of what we felt was in the basement. I lead out with the fact that I clocked the spirit life as Demonic and that posed a challenge: It was going to be more difficult to document much evidence "on-command" from a Demonic occupation. Demons don't do anything when anyone wishes them to -- especially to conveniently appear on camera.

While I was discussing the nature of the entities in the basement, the temperature of the air around dropped sharply. Being exposed for what they are is something Demons don't appreciate. It puts a crimp in their "ambush predator" style. The more I explained to the group what I'd found below, the more the cold bit into my flesh. Shortly thereafter, I jolted up off my chair as "something" sucker-punched me through the floor, right in the kidney. I let out a yelp. Recognizing what had happened, I mentioned it to the group (who was looking at me rather quizzically), and I continued onward.

Demons expect you to react. When you don't, they aren't sure how to proceed. And the last thing I wanted to demonstrate to them was that pain would be an effective way to get my attention. That always ends badly.

We finished our discussion and I accompanied the paranormal investigation group on one of the turns downstairs. I was actually more scared of getting spiders in my hair than I was of these Demonic pests, so I made sure to wear a hoodie – hood up.

The stairs creaked below our feet as we all shuffled downward. By the time I landed on the dirt floor below, I was not a happy camper. In fact, I was angry. I was mad that these low-vibration parasites had knocked me in the kidney, and mad that they banged on the floor a few days ago. I was even irritated that they put on the Dog and Pony Horror Show earlier that day. Never mind the incident I experienced upon first arriving at the home while using the restroom, which involved being verbally confronted while I was "freshening up". (Yes, that actually happened.) I was well and truly sick of these guys. At that juncture, I was in no way frightened of them. I'd had it with the bully tactics.

As such, I let them have it.

Once in the pitch black belly of that dank basement -- I let fly, verbally but mostly energetically. This made me feel better but didn't do much for the filming of paranormal phenomenon, as the Demonic entities stayed well out of my energy field while the Geyser blew. Wouldn't they be relishing in the negativity of my anger, you may ask? Well, not exactly. They eat suffering and fear. I was experiencing neither. Nothing says "Bright Light" like a Psychic responding to being energetically bullied.

In reaction to my tirade, they pushed back a little -- rocking a dangling ceiling light, manifesting a few really cold spots around us, and draining a few batteries on the camera. But, like any predator, they'd prefer to hunt the sick, not the strong. It was too much work. So they hissed off a couple of creepy EVPs caught on the Second Unit Director's camera mic while hiding in the rafters -- and stuck to the shadows until I went upstairs.

I made for a lousy buffet. Apparently, I was much more enticing to interact with while using the toilet.

The paranormal investigation group had more luck in catching the Demonic horde on camera when the basement was empty. They captured a black mass moving downstairs, and another black mass completely blocking the Infrared camera view as it was trained on the dripping grotto. (Finally, someone besides me was seeing that creepy black yuck in the basement.) During their investigation, they captured numerous disturbing EVPs, Coupled with what my camera crew was able to catch, we all accrued some of the best EVP's I've ever heard. Their group findings were all included in the film.

My film crew did finally succeed in capturing a solid entity on camera. In the attic, the spirit of a young, sickly boy was documented, frame by frame. Twisted and drained by years of being caught in the vacant ethers -- the child looked more ghoul than good boy.

One EVP in particular was a frightening stand-out. I found it accidently while scrolling through the footage seeking a particular shot. It was located on two cameras simultaneously – one belonging to the paranormal group, and one belonging to my film crew. A member of the paranormal group was standing at the base of the stairs, where I had initially viewed the first "man" in the apron and gloves. She was asking the entity to speak to her. In true form, the Demons could only remain silent in the darkness, pestered by humans, for so long.

Finally, the classic utterance was captured on dual cameras: "GET OUT!"

*Post Script*: The Montgomery House was blessed by the Cowlitz Indian Holy Man in a special ceremony that lasted nearly four hours. Though some human entities decided to stay in the home, the hundreds of Cowlitz souls attached to the land were freed. As the Holy Man raised the vibration in the house, all contrary Darkness was forced out. The next day, the basement felt like a whole new room as it had been energetically cleared of the Demonic activity. The paranormal investigation group left an infrared camera running in the black of the basement while the blessing was happening upstairs. Over a four hour period, the camera caught a cable being slowly tugged toward a doorway leading outside under the porch. It was as if the cable was caught up in some energetic tide, being swept along with the Darkness -- right out the door.

# 10
# BLOOD BY THE BAY
## WHERE: VACATION HOME
## LOCATION: NEWPORT, OR

It is said that more spirits are held to the sea than anywhere else. If we're talking sheer spiritual physics, there are many reasons for this. The greatest of these reasons is water. Water is an incredible spiritual semi-conductor. Think about dropping a hairdryer into a bathtub; that water pulls the electricity through the tub to lethal levels. Spirits, or souls, are actually a form of electricity. Just like a wall socket, Spirits emit EMF (Electro Magnetic Fields), which is why we see all the ghost hunters on television carrying around the same EMF readers used by your garden-variety electrician.

The deep tidal lull created by the sea is something with which our bodies naturally fall into rhythm. Again, there are many reasons for this, the greatest being the human brain's compulsion to lock onto the rhythm of the waves. During the 1940's, famed neurophysiologist William Gray Walter demonstrated that the brain's EEG activity – the alpha and beta waves -- mirrored the activity of flickering candlelight. This phenomenon was forever tagged as the brain's Frequency Following Response (FFR). The human brain's FFR is triggered in the same manner by the rhythmic crashing of waves. Add to the neurological stew the occurrence of white noise while seaside, the sound created by the waves crashing, and you have a frequency canvas that is the psychological equivalent of Novocain. White noise floods the brain with so much information that the brain doesn't feel obligated to have to sort it all out, so it goes offline for awhile to relax. While resting, the human brain is able to expand itself, applying more advanced methods of tapping the relationship between mind and body. While expanded in this altered state of consciousness, our brain is allowed to stray from its daily grind of brass-tacks Beta waves and be lifted into the daydream zone – the Alpha wave – or, depending on the individual, even the sixth-sense atmosphere of the Theta wave zone. Fall asleep by the sea and you may even achieve the Delta wave state, which is the slowest brain pattern and always present alongside reports of out-of-body experiences, such as astral travel.

The planet is designed to inspire humanity to reach its fullest potential. The ocean is the nervous system of the planet. It is our spiritual pacemaker. We are an extension of the oceans, having dragged ourselves on our fins from the womb of the salty brine that birthed the Homo Sapien. It should come as no surprise to anyone that the sea, therefore, is a place that beckons us not only in life, but in death.

One spring back 1994, my partner at the time, "Keira", and I headed out to Keira's family vacation home in Newport, Oregon. Newport had its back braced up against the wild and churning Pacific coastline yet its belly was nestled safely against Yaquina Bay. Keira's family home was an extremely modest two story cracker box beach bungalow that had been erected in the 1950's. The house sat high up on a ridge that overlooked the bay below. The terrain to the left of the home tumbled into a deep canyon whose bottom was punctuated by a trickle of water; the tributary's tenacity had whittled its own private resting place. Steep canyon shelves were wrapped for safekeeping in thickets of blackberry bushes, camouflaging the treacherous plummet.

It was in that canyon that many years ago Keira's brother had found an ancient stone mortar and pestle, giving hint to the prehistoric Native Americans who once took shelter there. The pestle itself had been carved into the shape of a whale. As boys do, they played with the artifact until it was commandeered by Keira's father, who, as an attorney, placed it somewhere safe. Keira later learned that a mortar and pestle of this detailed nature would be a piece used in high spiritual ceremonies. It was likely the canyon next door had been used as a burial site. The artifact itself was most common for ceremonial materials used by tribes such as the Chinook Indians of Portland around 1400 AD.

The inaccessible canyon held many secrets, including a nauseating stench that lasted for such a lengthy duration that Keira's father was moved to mention that he felt the cause of the stench was a human body that had been dumped down the ravine. Considering the dangerous cliff walls had claimed many animals over the years, even

Keira knew the difference between a dead deer and this rancid smell. She recounted later that the acrid ripe-rotten stench took weeks to subside and happened to coincide with the Green River killings in the 1980's. It went unspoken that tangled deep into the canyon could be one of Gary Leon Ridgway's 71 unclaimed victims. It turned out that this line of thinking could have been more factual than fanciful. Gary Leon Ridgway confessed to more murders than any other serial killer in America. Though Ridgway dumped the bodies of most victims in King County, WA, it was documented later that he did occasionally dispose of bodies in Oregon in order to throw off local authorities. Ted Bundy also admitted to several Oregon murders and there would be no better place to dispose of a body than within the belly of the blackberry-tangled chasm. Eventually the relentless Northwest rain washed away the mysterious stink – but not the macabre memory.

As we drove up to the home, I could not help note the simplicity with which the house had been maintained considering the multi-million dollar properties that sprang up all along the high ridge line. Keira's family home was the very last of its generation, standing resolute in its silence – a testament to quality time spent with family over tattered board games during a simple family weekend getaway. The palatial mansions that swallowed lot after lot next door knew not what it meant to dress in the same flowered wallpaper since 1962, or wear the shoes of the glue-backed short-pile office carpeting that begged to be filled with sand. So busy were they to be the view – many of the grand homes themselves forgot how to enjoy the view.

The narrow gravel driveway crunched under the car tires and the modest house came into view. Glancing out at us through a small window on the second floor was a woman who looked to be in her 40's. She had a very traditional 1950's hairstyle, caramel brown, shorter bangs with the flipped curls bobby-pinned into place. We met eyes. She wasn't smiling but she had a pleasant expression on her face. She seemed to have been expecting us, and now satisfied that we had arrived, she turned from the window and walked away. I had no idea that we were going to be sharing the home for the weekend with the rest of Keira's family. I was looking forward to meeting this woman.

"Hey," I broke the silence, "who is that older lady with the brown hair who was looking out the upstairs window?"

"Oh," replied Keira, "that's Beatrice."

"Is Beatrice your aunt?" I asked.

"No," answered Keira, not skipping a beat while she placed the car in park. "Beatrice is my dad's first wife. She's dead."

I looked back up to the window above. I should have been shocked, except the look in the woman's eye was so peaceful and her hairstyle was so antiquated that it just made sense.

"Okay," I mused as I unhitched my seatbelt and opened the door. "Are there any other ghosts in this house I need to know about?"

"Just Julie," answered Keira as she started pulling her suitcases from the backseat. "She sometimes gets protective of me when I first bring friends here."

"And Julie would be...?" I replied as I joined in on the luggage.

"Julie is my sister – my dad's first daughter, with Beatrice. She fell out of a tree when she was little and suffered a brain injury. She died right before I was born. She shouldn't give you any trouble though."

I suppose it was that nonchalant manner in which Keira relayed this information that allowed me to remain so unaffected in the wake of just laying eyes on a solid manifestation of an entity. Obviously Keira had seen this "Beatrice" as well. My consciousness was still attempting to make sense of what I'd just witnessed. I was actually surprised that Keira was so matter-of-fact in her retelling of these stories, considering Keira was not a spiritual person, and we never talked of ghosts. But Keira surely did not seem one bit upset by the fact that a manifested ghost was wandering the upstairs of the beach home. Even though I didn't truly have a "handle" on my spiritual abilities just yet – the confidence in which Keira rattled off the inconceivable instilled me with a sense of calm.

I looked back up to the empty window. "Julie and Beatrice. Got it."

We loaded our suitcases into the house and the interior matched the exterior: Floral wall paper in the kitchen, small, low-hanging cabinets, an old refrigerator and thick metal stove with a living room equipped with floor-to-ceiling 1960's mod light fixtures on tension poles. The drapes were rubber-backed 1950's specials made of a thick earth tone weave, the rubber cracking with age and stained orange from whatever mildew had taken up residence after 40 years on the Oregon coast. Each room in the house was tiny, and if this same residence had been located in my home state of Montana, it would have been instantly recognizable on the inside as a weekend get-away cabin. The ground floor consisted of the kitchen, "living room", and a "reading room". The three bedrooms and the one bath were located upstairs. The place was cozy, though extremely cold, as the weekend heat had not yet been kicked on.

We hauled our bags to the foot of the stairs, which was in the kitchen.

"Be careful going up," mentioned Keira. "These stairs are steep."

She wasn't kidding. Not only were they extremely steep, but the staircase was very narrow. Like everything else in this compact sea-side cottage, it had been miniaturized. We both turned sideways to drag up the bags, careful to lift each foot high onto the tall steps. Keira had neglected to mention that not only was the staircase steep, and narrow, but each step itself was quite tall.

As we ascended, the ether changed. I figured that the creepy sensation hanging in the air was likely a by-product of the claustrophobic feeling that came about while being pinched in the narrow staircase.

I told myself that this was the root of the emotion anyway, because again, at this time in my life (my early 20's) I really wasn't into the paranormal, past a fascination with ghost stories around the campfire. Looking back, I find it hard to believe that I was not more clinically curious about the Unknown, considering the enormous amount of paranormal activity with which I was beset my entire life. Perhaps this "dismissal" of the obvious on my part was a coping mechanism. Or perhaps it was due to the fact that I simply assumed that everyone else was experiencing the paranormal to the degree I was, and ergo, I didn't see the point in banging the gong of the obvious. Whatever the truth may have been, it didn't occur to me to mention to Keira that in climbing the stairs, we had crossed into an entirely different spiritual environment.

We took up residence in the bedroom directly at the top of the stairs. The doorway was immediately left of the landing where the staircase emptied onto the second floor. This bedroom had been Keira's when she was young. On one side, it had a wonderful view of the harbor below. The other window looked out over the bramble-riddled ravine. We tossed our bags on the bed and prepped to go out to grab some legendary Newport clam chowder.

I needed to freshen up my make-up, so I headed to the bathroom, which involved crossing in front of the head of the staircase and hanging a right. As I turned into the tiny open hallway upstairs, I could not help but allow my gaze to fall upon the window through which Beatrice had greeted us upon our arrival. It came as no surprise that there was a window box complete with seat cushions beneath the window itself. I could feel someone sitting there as I stood quietly in front of the bathroom door. Though I could not see her at this time, I knew Beatrice was there, that pleasant, resigned look likely on her face. I felt this nudge from her, as if she were saying, "Go ahead, go to the

# Barjon's Books

223 North 29th St
Billings, MT 59101
(406) 252-4398

Cust: **None**

07-Oct-16 9:16p     Clerk: sumari
Trans # 10073517     Reg 2

1478181109     *True Tales Of The Tr*
   1 @ $17.95        .      $17.95  *

|  | Sub-total: | $17.95 |
|  | Total: | **$17.95** |

* *Non-Tax Items*
   *Items: 1*        *Units: 1*

Payment Via:

CASH               $20.00

Change (Cash)       **$2.05**

RETURN POLICY:

Stones, Oils, Herbs, Used Books & Decks,
Sale and Layaway Items are non-returnable.

All other items must returned within 14 days of
purchase, must be accompanied by the original
receipt, must be unopened and in saleable
condition.

Refunds from checks will be issued 30 days
from the date of purchase in the form of a
business check.

restroom and finish your business. Keira is waiting and I live here. I'm sure we'll see each other later."

I smiled, satisfied with the motherly nag from the other side to get a move on. I got my make-up on, and we headed down to the waterfront for some of the best clam chowder I've ever had.

We were joined in the house that weekend by several friends of Keira's, who had all been part of her high school gang. It was a great deal of fun, hanging out with the group and laughing about this or that adventure they once had.

Late that night, after a full day of exchanging stories and eating until we popped, it was time to head to bed. Keira's friends took the other two bedrooms and we all turned in. The house was vacuum quiet at night. It was quite peaceful. That is, until one left the bedroom.

As usual, I had to use the powder room in the middle of the night. I got up and went to the door, which was closed, and upon opening it, I was hit with such a high radiant wall of EMF that I literally took a step back from the doorway. I stared into the static darkness. The hallway was illuminated with the grey glow from the moon. Though I could see nothing – something was there. The door across the landing was closed. The room contained one of Keira's sleeping pals, as did the other bedroom upstairs, whose door was also closed. In the far corner the bathroom door stood open.

I peeked out from around the door jam and stared down the dark staircase, which was directly to my right. It was a narrow, black tunnel, whose mouth at the bottom had an eerie gray glow. I was unnerved by the feeling of something standing in the dark of the tunnel – something waiting until I crossed over the doorjamb to rush up the stairs in an unseen flurry.

This was not Beatrice.

No matter how spooky the scenario, nature was still calling. I left the bedroom door open and quickly darted into the hallway. I made it past the mouth of the staircase without being accosted, grabbing the banister ball to-hang a quick right toward the restroom. Before I could even head down the hall – there it was, glued to my back like a cold blanket of creep. Something had rushed up from the staircase and was looming large behind me. I didn't dare turn around. I zipped into the bathroom and threw on the light. The thing would not follow me into the bathroom, perhaps dissuaded by the hum of the old, poorly-grounded light fixture. Spirits, being energy, are at times disturbed by the electrical current flowing through the walls and light bulbs throughout a home.

I stood toward the back of the bathroom, staring into the blackness in the hallway. I couldn't see anything, but I could feel whatever this was, just standing still, its "toes" pressed up against the wooden lip of the bathroom tile. I snapped forward and closed the old five paneled door. I really didn't want to be glared at while using the restroom.

I took care of business and realized that I had to once again cross back through the hallway to return to the bedroom. I opened the bathroom door quickly – I didn't want to give this thing any time to hide, if indeed it was out in the hall. Upon opening the door, I could no longer sense its presence directly outside, but the upstairs radiated with its energy. It was around. I just couldn't find it. I took a breath, clicked off the old light, and half-ran the short distance back to the bedroom.

Just as before, about halfway into the hall, this thing rushed up behind me and pressed against my back. This time, I had a better picture of whatever this was, in my mind's eye. It wasn't big, actually. It was shorter than I was, and I'm 5' 5". It was a young girl around the age of nine or ten. She was floating several inches off the ground, and black, like a disembodied shadow. It was absolutely furious I was there. It had its shoulder against me, then its belly, then its hands, frantic to press into me. I learned later on in my life that as a Medium, or someone wired to be a swinging saloon door between the here and the hereafter, spirits attempt to enter a body from two places – either from a chakra point on the back which is located between the shoulder blades, or from the front, at exactly the same spot only located mid-sternum.

I could feel this thing shoving me from the back, and the more it shoved, the faster I ran. I grabbed a hold of the banister ball to hang a left and swing back into the bedroom. Just three more feet and I was home free. This thing seemed to hang in the hallway. It was a good thing that I had a hold of the banister, as just as I stepped in front of the black, plummeting stairwell, the entity swung to my right and pushed as hard as it could.

The pressure on my right shoulder was obvious and I slid a few inches to the left, toward the top of the steps; this nasty-tempered thing was trying to push me down the stairs. I had more forward momentum going for me than it had the ability to manipulate solid matter, so I tripped into the bedroom and quickly closed the door.

I could feel it on the other side, silently screaming in defeat, its hands balled in fists at its side.

This was going to be an interesting weekend.

The next morning I recounted the whole adventure to Keira, whose response was: "Oh. That's Julie. I'm sorry. Sometimes she gets jealous. But she's usually not that bad."

Really?

Keira told me she'd have a talk with her. I suggested some energetic Depakote. She told me that that wasn't too far off, as Julie's head injury had left her disoriented and prone to outbursts. I came to find out that when she was a young girl, the injury that she incurred falling out of the tree would leave her developmentally delayed, and shorten her life. She would live to be barely 30, but with the mental capacity of a child. Julie died after Beatrice, who was diagnosed with fatal colon cancer.

Keira's father lost his first wife and daughter to two separate tragedies, one right after the other. With two sons to raise, he married Keira's mother and started a new family. Life was tough back then. Keira's mother, who was also a nurse, took wonderful care of Julie and the young boys until Julie's death. Then, of course, Keira came along.

I couldn't help but wonder whether the room in which we were staying at the seaside cottage had originally been Julie's. Whatever the case – Julie was just not happy that I was there. And it made sense if she truly was a possessive and jealous ghost. Here I was, another girl spending a lot of time with Keira. That had to be a rub for Julie, who never got to spend a day with her sister in this lifetime.

It also made sense to me, if Julie was still there, why Beatrice was still there. Perhaps Beatrice tarried behind, keeping an eye on her daughter. Keira informed me that Beatrice and Julie remained at the Newport house to greet her father who would make regular weekend treks to the property, many times without company. In some way, Keira thought, her father held them to the property by seeking their memory in the time he would spend there. It is not uncommon for the spirits of deceased people to stay in this incarnation, rather than to cross over, on behalf of a loved one who appears to need them.

The more I spent time in the home, the more I realized that the home itself had a very thin veil between the here and the hereafter. Though very quaint, there was most definitely a subtle other-wordly feeling to the place, as if the home was out of space and time. This effect was so understated that it wasn't something one would notice right away, without blaming the sensation on the *My Three Sons* styled furniture and classic 60's light fixtures. But truly, the house sat on a rift between the ethers. Whether naturally created or created by great human grief, it was through this rift that spirit life would roam.

I asked Keira if anything scary ever happened to her in the home. She said no, but did tell me of a recurring dream that she'd suffered with every time she stayed in the home as a child. The dream only occurred in the Newport home, and consisted of her being upstairs in bed and then smelling smoke. Alarmed, she'd jump up and run onto the hallway on the landing only to see that the home was ablaze. She'd start down the stairs in an effort to escape but saw that a washing machine, engulfed in flames, had been pushed up against the foot of the stairwell, blocking the only way out. The dream would always end with her panicking and waking up – trapped to burn to death in a home she could not escape.

I've often times wondered if she was Psychically picking up on Julie's experience in the home. Though Julie was not involved in a fire, the feeling of being trapped upstairs in a house would mirror the anger and desperation I felt coming off of the entity. I would be very interested to know if there ever was a fire in the home, or on the property prior to the home being built.

The next night, I was dreading the stand-off with Julie. I had hoped that pep-talk Keira delivered to her deceased sister would lessen the sibling's vitriol. Ascending the narrow stairs to turn in, I could feel the cross into the upstairs ethers and ignored the sensation. We turned into bed without incident.

Again during the night I found it necessary to visit the restroom. I was prepped for the experience this time, and braced for the wall of weirdness. I opened the door and zipped to the bathroom, enduring the very same tag-along entity right at my back. This time, in a hurry to use the restroom, I left the door open with the light on realizing everyone else in the home was asleep with their doors closed and knowing that the entity wouldn't cross into the bathroom.

Leaving the door open was a mistake.

As I was busy using the facilities, I looked toward the hallway. In the doorway, just to the side of the hallway, was a perfectly blacker-than-black shadow – just standing there. It was small in frame and hovered about six inches off the floor. Either that or its ankles and feet simply went invisible. I went cold, and found it difficult to finish what I had started, but I managed. As I got up to wash my hands, I kept a sharp eye on this thing. It hovered outside the doorjamb for quite some time, looking as though it was shifting from one foot to the other. I was making sure to keep an eye on it. I took a split second to reach for the towel and dry my hands, and when I looked up – it was gone.

Crud. Now it could be anywhere.

I could still feel it upstairs. I glanced out the bathroom door to the bedroom door in the other corner of the hall, which couldn't have been more then 16 feet away. I was in full-tilt dread over having to go out in to that hallway where I just saw a black figure, standing and staring at me. But unless I planned on sleeping in the bathroom all night – which wouldn't be recommended considering we had other house guests -- I had to make a run for it.

And make a run I did.

In one movement, I snapped off the light and scurried down the hallway toward the bedroom. Suddenly, the hallway appeared to tilt as if someone had twisted the entire house. I was incredibly dizzy, and I slowed my pace to brace myself against the wall to my right as I fell into it. I realized what this entity was doing. It was trying to knock me off my game before I got myself to the head of the stairwell. I knew what this was all about – it was about getting me shoved to the bottom of those narrow, neck-breaking stairs.

Despite the funhouse effect of the floor twisting, thanks to an incredibly jacked-up EMF field which this entity seemed to activating somehow, I made it to the banister, where I grabbed a firm hold on the ball to steady myself. The floor, which had been appearing to "tilt" right, suddenly swiveled and tilted left. I slid across the floor as the house attempted to dump me straight down the stairwell. With my other hand I grabbed the antique doorknob on the bedroom door. I was suspended between two points, my body leaning heavily over the plummeting stairway. In this bizarre split second, I recall thinking that the house couldn't actually be tilting because I could hear no creaking or the crashing of drawers falling out of dressers. I recall telling myself to stay calm and to not let go of the banister until I opened the door. I told myself that somehow, this ghost had to be affecting my inner ear – it had to be – and was creating the illusion of the floor tipping. That really didn't explain my body dangling over the stairwell. But it was the best I had at that moment.

I flung the bedroom door open and threw myself across the threshold. The floor inside the bedroom was instantly level, as was the floor in the hallway where I'd been slipping down the stairs. I slammed the door and jumped into bed. Keira stirred, but didn't wake.

The next morning was all about me telling Keira the details of the Amityville Horror that had transpired the previous evening. She listened, and again, she apologized for Julie, saying that they'd never encountered such activity in the home before.

Well lucky me.

That last day we were to be in Newport, we played at the beach and had a glorious time. The night fell upon us, and one by one our house guests disappeared upstairs to their respective bedrooms. I wasn't sharing my wild encounters with anyone else in the home because none of the other guests reported any bizarre activity – except for "Jack", who had later claimed that on the first night of his stay, someone went through his suitcase and had strewn clothing all over his room. He blamed another house guest who was a notorious prankster for the deed, though she denied it.

That third night I was prepared. We walked up the frightening staircase and the ether didn't seem as bad. I was surprised but thought perhaps the ghost had given everything she had the night before. Upon realizing she wasn't going to get me down the stairs, she backed off.

Keira and I went to sleep. As usual, I was awakened in the middle of the night with the need to use the restroom, but I went into a mind-over-matter zone with my body, having no intention of actually going back out into the hallway. I rolled over on my side and started back to sleep.

Before I could nod back off again, I felt my head slowly being depressed into the pillow as if someone had two invisible hands on the side of my face and was slowly pressing downward. I couldn't feel the hands, but I definitely felt the pressure and I could hear the down quills inside the pillow crackling. My eyes popped open and surely enough, I could see the pillow slowly swallowing my face.

I didn't move, nor did I scream, but instead stayed quiet, seeing what else would happen. Though it was a disconcerting feeling, there was something relaxing about the pressure, and obviously, it was a slow and deliberate push, so whatever was doing it didn't have enough moxie to snap the pillow out from beneath my head and smother me beneath it. My head was held pressed down into the pillow until my eyes had been open for some time looking around the room. Then, it was released. Without the pressure, my head popped back up as the down pillow's stuffing pushed back.

It was then that I felt a warm trickling over my top lip and down my chin. I reached up to my mouth and encountered a warm slick – I looked at my hand and the liquid appeared to be dark black in the dimly lit room. Good lord, I had a nosebleed! And not just any nosebleed, but a real gusher. I could feel it pouring out of my nose and down my face. It was splattering my t-shirt and when I looked back on the pillow, it had left a massive puddle. I could hear something knocking outside my own consciousness, saying: "You really need to go to the bathroom."

I couldn't believe it. When I had ignored the "prompt" to use the rest room that night, Julie had given me a nosebleed to get me to go back out into that hallway. She wanted her last chance at shoving me down those stairs.

My nose was exploding everywhere. I cupped my nose and looked for something to place over my face to catch this spew, not wanting to get any blood on Keira who was sleeping next to me. I lunged over the side of the bed and snapped a T-shirt up off the floor, pressing it to my face.

In all this commotion, Keira woke up.

"What's the matter?" she asked.

"My nose is bleeding all over the place," I said, the t-shirt pressed over my face. I could feel the warm blood filling up the cotton in my hand.

"What? Oh, no!" she answered.

"Be careful, it's all over the bed," I mentioned.

I was wondering how much blood I was going to lose. I could feel the large patch of blood cooling stickily on my t-shirt against my chest. But I'd be damned if I was going to go out into the hallway. If this entity could give me a nosebleed this severe, chances are, that night she'd manage to chuck me down the stairwell by the scruff of my neck. Whether or not Keira and I would need to inflate a life-raft to row to safety on the river of blood spewing from my face – I was not heading to the bathroom, and crossing in front of that staircase.

I reached over to turn on the light to really survey the damage, whose black stains were easily visible in the dim moonlight. The light clicked on.

There, on the pillow, on the sheets, on my night shirt, and filling the t-shirt I had pressed against my face – was absolutely nothing.

I was stunned.

I frantically pulled sheets apart from blankets and turned the pillow over.

"I swear to God, Keira, my nose was bleeding all over the place," I insisted as I stared at perfectly clean sheets.

Keira stared at me, and stared at the bedding. She knew I wouldn't have made that up. She looked frightened, and confused. My gushing nosebleed had mysteriously vanished. I had felt it, from the trickle down my chin to the warmth on my skin to the slime on my fingers. I smelled it, and tasted it, and I'd seen it. And it was gone.

I sat quietly for a moment, and realized the entity's game plan. Julie had somehow created a phantom nosebleed just like she'd created the tilt in the floor that almost pitched me down the stairs. She wouldn't harm me in the room where Keira was present. But she would go through great lengths to get me to leave the room in order to remove what she considered to be a menace from her home.

We slept with the light on until the sun came up.

The next morning, I really had to use the restroom. And I did so without incident. We said our goodbyes to our houseguests and loaded up our belongings into the car. I looked at the house over my shoulder from outside, glancing at the window upstairs where Beatrice had initially made herself known. Beatrice was not there. I couldn't help but wonder if she were somewhere else, giving Julie the ethereal spanking of her lifetime.

As we strapped ourselves into the car and backed away, the gravel crunching beneath the tires, and I knew that would be the last time I would ever see the Newport house. There was a melancholy that befell the property as we left – perhaps its residents realizing their quiet and fate until someone else would come back to keep them company.

I often thought of Julie and Beatrice. I had sincerely hoped that the specter that gave me so much trouble was indeed not Julie – but in truth, my gut confirmed the identity of the ghost. I wanted Julie to be at peace – and maybe she was, playing with her mother in a fond childhood home. Perhaps she just didn't like me.

And hey – that's fair.

It would be five years later in 1999 that my attention would be brought back to the Newport house. Keira and I had relocated to Montana and by this time, were no longer partners but had stayed very good friends. Keira had accompanied our mutual friend "Wilma" out to the coast for a fun weekend trip. Wilma was much older, and was fun to hang around. Of course, they stayed in Keira's family home – the Newport house -- while visiting the Oregon coast. I didn't think twice about the stay, as Wilma didn't believe in ghosts, nor would she ever discuss them or even entertain the idea that a ghost would cross her path.

I received a phone call at around 1:25 one morning while Keira and Wilma were away. I checked the caller ID – this was back in the day before I had a cell phone – and the number was Wilma's. I thought this was odd, considering how late it was. Upon answering the phone, I encountered a terrified Wilma who recounted to me with a trembling voice how she and Keira had gone to the beach, only to return home to the locked Newport house to find that the clothes in her suitcase – once neatly packed – had been ruffled through and pulled out into the bed.

Julie must've not been too crazy about Wilma either.

I calmed Wilma down and told her that yes, there was a ghost, but no, she didn't need to be afraid of her. I didn't dare tell her the nosebleed story. Wilma didn't really feel better by the time she got off the phone with me. I got Keira on the horn who was laughing about the whole incident. Poor Wilma never did quite recover from that one, I don't think. They left the next day.

As the years passed, Keira's father had failing health and was no longer able to make trips to the coast. The home became more difficult to maintain as an infestation of rats in the old walls was nearly impossible to eradicate. Exterminator after exterminator would pump the walls full of poison and still, the rats would thrive. Interestingly enough, properties that sit on ground prone to paranormal issues will also be prone to pests – roaches, spiders, snakes, and vermin. Between the lack of visitations to the home and the infestation of disease-carrying rodents, the tough decision was made to sell the property and the fate of the Newport house was eventually tossed into the hands of new owners. Keira was deeply saddened over the loss of the home, and even more saddened to hear that due to the never-ending laundry list of maladies – the new owners razed the house. It was not long afterward that Keira's father passed away as well.

My wish for both Beatrice and Julie was that they would have greeted Keira's father on the other side, and moved from that property high on the ridge overlooking the bay. We have such a profound ability to hold those that we love to us, even after those who we love depart this earthly place. I'm not insinuating that Keira's father was solely responsible for holding his loved ones to the Newport property. I believe very much that Beatrice wanted to be there, remembering the home as a fond family bonding experience. Yet it is so very important that we allow our loved ones to pass on, keeping in mind the awareness that we, too, will see them again one day.

From Newport, Oregon to Hardin, Montana, from Seattle, Washington to Tucson, Arizona, I had seen and felt and touched more types of paranormal phenomenon than I would ever have time to recount in any one book. I'd learned so much about myself and about the world beyond -- a world that defies our five senses -- that it would forever change my perception of our known Universe. I'd realized that for every terrifying ghost I'd encountered, there were five more, all of whom were happy to be helpful. I'd learned for every Demon lurking in the darkness, there were fifty Angels ready to be of service. I'd learned that no matter what I'd learned -- there would always be more to learn.

Life is fragile, and it is spectacular. It is fickle and unfair. It is just and unjust. It is both parts miraculous and terrifying. There is no single key that unlocks the secrets of the Universe. Yet together, we are the key. Together, we decode the whispers of those who have gone on before us. Together, we decipher the roar of the earth beneath our feet. Alone, we are numbed by the silence. Together, we listen. We live day to day. Our heart lives love to love. And our soul lives life to life. Our choices in this physical incarnation have spiritual repercussions. We must forgive those whose actions we don't understand. To do less tethers the spirit -- ours and theirs. We must embrace those who are in pain, for their suffering is our suffering, stamped into the ethers for all time. Our reality is only that: Ours. We are immersed in the spiritual world as a pebble is swallowed by the sea.

*I am you, and you are me.*
*Therein lies the mystery.*

Made in the USA
San Bernardino, CA
01 March 2016